J. S. Bach's Major Works for Voices and Instruments

A Listener's Guide

Melvin P. Unger

The Scarecrow Press, Inc.
Lanham, Maryland • Toronto • Oxford
2005

SCARECROW PRESS, INC.

Published in the United States of America
by Scarecrow Press, Inc.
A wholly owned subsidiary of
The Rowman & Littlefield Publishing Group, Inc.
4501 Forbes Boulevard, Suite 200, Lanham, Maryland 20706
www.scarecrowpress.com

PO Box 317
Oxford
OX2 9RU, UK

British Library Cataloguing in Publication Information Available

Library of Congress Cataloging-in-Publication Data

Unger, Melvin P., 1950–
    J.S. Bach's major works for voices and instruments : a listener's guide / Melvin
P. Unger.
        p. cm.
    Includes bibliographical references and index.
    ISBN 0-8108-5298-5 (pbk. : alk. paper)
    1. Bach, Johann Sebastian, 1685–1750. Choral music. I. Title.
    ML410.B13U54 2005
    782.5'092—dc22
                                        2004024286

TOC-P

⊖™ The paper used in this publication meets the minimum requirements of
American National Standard for Information Sciences—Permanence of
Paper for Printed Library Materials, ANSI/NISO Z39.48-1992.
Manufactured in the United States of America.

For Jeremy, Tim, and Andrew

Contents

Preface

This book is designed for the reader who wishes to better understand the dramatic thrust of Bach's four major works for choir and orchestra: the *Christmas Oratorio*, the *St. John Passion*, the *St. Matthew Passion*, and the *Mass in B Minor*. It is based on extensive program notes prepared for the Baldwin-Wallace College Bach Festival, an annual event with a tradition of presenting the four masterworks in cyclical fashion going back to the festival's founding in 1933 by Albert Riemenschneider. The book addresses Bach's four compositions as utterances heard *in time*. Giving priority to the salient auditory and dramatic features of the music, it guides the listener through each work, movement by movement, with an integrated presentation of commentary and text translation that pays particular attention to the interaction of text and music, and suggests reasons for Bach's musical choices.

Each work is presented with a general introduction. The texts (with parallel, non-rhyming translations) then follow movement by movement, interspersed with commentary. The libretti are rendered according to the new critical edition of Bach's works (*Neue Bach-Ausgabe*), which sometimes employs old German spellings (e.g., "frohlokket"). To identify Scriptural texts within the libretti, italics are used; to identify chorale (hymn) texts, bold print is used.

Introduction

In a report datelined May 29, 1723, a Hamburg newspaper reported:

> This past Saturday at noon, four wagons loaded with household
> goods arrived here from Cöthen; they belonged to the former
> Princely Capellmeister there, now called to Leipzig as Cantor
> Figuralis. He himself arrived with his family on 2 carriages at 2
> o'clock and moved into the newly renovated apartment in the St.
> Thomas School.[1]

Upon coming to Leipzig from Cöthen in 1723 Johann Sebastian Bach
assumed the most prominent music position in the city, a post with dual
titles and roles. As "Cantor" Bach was responsible for the music education
of the boys enrolled at the St. Thomas School. As "Director musices" he
was responsible for the musical activity of the city, above all for providing
music in its two main churches: the churches of St. Nicholas and St.
Thomas. Bach arrived in Leipzig on May 22, 1723, and began his duties
as director of music in the Leipzig churches on May 30, the first Sunday
after Trinity. During the next twenty-seven years, until his death in 1750,
he wrote most of his vocal works: almost all of the extant cantatas (some
two hundred and fifteen), the *Magnificat*, the *St. Matthew Passion*, the
Christmas Oratorio, and the *Mass in B Minor*. The *St. John Passion*, too,
belongs to the Leipzig period. While it may have been written in the
months just prior to Bach's move to Leipzig, it was evidently written with
the new position in mind, and was first performed in Leipzig during
Bach's first year there (April 7, 1724).

Note

1. *Staats- und Gelehrte Zeitung*, cited in *Bach-Dokumente*, 2:104 (no. 138). An English translation may be found in Hans T. David and Arthur Mendel, eds., *The New Bach Reader: A Life of Johann Sebastian Bach in Letters and Documents*. Revised and enlarged by Christoph Wolff (New York: W. W. Norton, 1998), 106 (no. 102).

1

Christmas Oratorio (BWV 248)

The historical origins of the oratorio can be traced back to the devotional exercises of the Congregazione dell'Oratorio, a religious society in Rome founded by St. Philip Neri (1515–95). Preferring popular styles of sacred music, the society welcomed the adaptation of operatic style for sacred use in its meetings. The works that resulted were called "oratorios," named after the "oratory" (i.e., prayer chapel) in which they were performed. Soon the term was widely accepted throughout Europe as the designation for a sacred musical drama. While they usually employed neither costumes nor scenery, oratorios borrowed the forms of contemporary opera: recitative, aria, and chorus.

Only three Bach "oratorios" have come down to us, each of which he entitled "Oratorium": the *Easter Oratorio*, BWV 249 (1725), the *Ascension Oratorio*, BWV 11 (1735), and the *Christmas Oratorio*, BWV 248 (1734–35). Of these, the *Christmas Oratorio* is the only one intended to be performed on six different days, though it forms a unified whole. Put simply, it consists of six separate cantatas to be spread out over the "thirteen days" of Christmas (the "twelve days of Christmas" in the Western church calendar are counted from Christmas Day to the *beginning* of Epiphany).

I. The birth of Christ and the angels' announcement to the shepherds: First Day of Christmas (December 25)

II. The revelation of Christ's birth to the shepherds: Second Day of Christmas (December 26)

III.   The adoration of the shepherds: Third Day of Christmas (December 27)

IV.   The naming of Jesus: Feast of the Circumcision (January 1)

V.   The arrival of the wise men at Herod's court: First Sunday of the New Year

VI.   The adoration and return of the wise men: Feast of the Epiphany (January 6)

Overall unity is provided by the recurring key of D major and its related "festive" orchestration (which includes trumpets and drums—see especially Cantatas I, III, and VI), and the appearance of the same familiar hymn tune near the beginning and at the end of the work.

Spread out over six days in Bach's day, the parts would each have been performed in the cantata's usual liturgical position, that is, between the Gospel reading and the creed, after which came the sermon. Normally, cantata texts related directly to the prescribed scriptural Gospel lesson. The *Christmas Oratorio* represents an interesting departure from the expected pattern, for three of its six cantatas quote from lessons one day removed from their own: Parts II and III each quote from the Gospel of the day preceding their own, while Part V quotes from the lesson of the day following. Since the Gospel lesson was always read immediately prior to the performance of the cantata (often called the *Hauptmusik*, that is, the "principal music"), one can imagine a certain puzzlement on the part of the listeners, who first heard the day's lesson read or chanted, then the Gospel of the previous day (or coming day) sung. Why were these texts deliberately shifted in this manner?

Probably, this disengagement from the schedule of lessons was motivated by a desire for a unified and compelling story. By extending the first Gospel to the second day and shifting the second Gospel to the third day, the librettist could omit the third lesson (John 1:1–14), which is not narrative in the usual sense and would have stalled the forward thrust of the story. Furthermore, by dividing the Gospel for Epiphany (the sixth and last of the series) between the fifth and sixth days, the poet could omit the account of Mary and Joseph's flight to Egypt, which in fifth place could not logically precede the appearance of the magi. The resulting libretto is a unified oratorio cycle.

However, nonsynchronization between lessons and libretto may be justified in another way as well. The temporal shifts effectively portray a duality between "recalling" and "anticipating," an important theme in the libretto. Thus, movements 30–32 (in one of the two cantatas that quote previous days' lessons) stress the former (e.g., "Maria behielt alle diese

Worte"—Mary retained all these words, "mein Herz soll es bewahren"—
My heart shall preserve it); and 51–52 (in the cantata that quotes from the
subsequent lesson), the latter (e.g., "Wann wird die Zeit erscheinen"—
When shall that time come?).

One striking feature of the *Christmas Oratorio* is the remarkably
frequent appearance (even for Bach) of chorales. Fifteen in all, their
disposition is symmetrical: three in each of Parts I, II, and III; two in each
of Parts IV, V, and VI.

Part	Movement
I.	5, 7 11
II.	12, 17, 23
III.	28, 33, 35
IV.	38 (continued in 40), 42
V.	46, 53
VI.	59, 64

These movements, even if they were not actually sung by the congregation
in Bach's day, should be understood as corporate statements of affirmation
and identification.

Perhaps the most musically significant aspect of the *Christmas
Oratorio* is its extensive use of parody—that is to say, for much of it,
Bach reused music he had composed earlier for other occasions. Recycling
music (parody technique, as it is now called) was common in the Baroque
period. By carefully matching emotional sentiment with musical gestures,
composers could reuse music they had written earlier. Such economy of
means was particularly appealing if the original occasion was a nonrecurring event. To be sure, some modern listeners have wondered about
Bach's tendency to recycle secular music for sacred use. This is what he
did in the *Christmas Oratorio*: much of it is borrowed from Cantatas 213,
214, and 215, all congratulatory cantatas for the Elector of Saxony and his
family. (In the sixth part, Bach borrowed from a recently composed—but
no longer extant—sacred cantata.)

A number of explanations have been put forth to justify Bach's reuse
of previous secular works: the common musical language of the day
included stock rhetorical figures, which could be used in any number of
contexts provided the affect was the same; the secular-sacred antithesis
was not nearly so pronounced in Lutheran orthodoxy as in present-day
Western culture; Bach was frugal in nature and liked to exploit all latent
potential of musical material (especially in cases where a cantata had been
written for a specific, nonrecurring event). All of these arguments have

merit. In any case, Bach's technical mastery in refitting music to a new text is such that the new version is often as convincing as the original. Furthermore, the newly composed recitatives and inserted chorales show considerably more imagination than might be expected. These provide additional levels of contemplation (a role normally assumed by the arias of an oratorio—although exceptions can be found, particularly in the *St. Matthew Passion*), and help draw the listener into progressively deeper involvement and identification with the events of the unfolding story.

Part I

Taken from a cantata composed a year earlier (1733) for the birthday celebration of Electress Maria Josepha of Saxony, the opening movement of the *Christmas Oratorio* retains its original royal air. Like the opening choruses of Parts III and VI it employs the "festive" orchestra, that is, trumpets and timpani have been added to the usual flutes, oboes, strings, and continuo. Particularly noteworthy (and unusual) is the very opening, which features a timpani solo. The reason for Bach's choice becomes clear when we consider the original words: "Tönet, ihr Pauken! Ershallet, Trompeten!" ("Sound, ye drums! Resound, ye trumpets!"). Though here applied to the child in the manger, the celebratory, regal mood is nevertheless fitting.

1. Chorus (Parody of BWV 214/1)

Jauchzet, frohlokket,	Rejoice and exult,
auf, preiset die Tage,	awake, praise these days;
rühmet, was heute	extol what God
der Höchste getan!	has accomplished today.
Lasset das Zagen,	Be not faint-hearted,
verbannet die Klage,	forsake lamentation,
stimmet voll Jauchzen	raise your voices with gladness
und Fröhlichkeit an!	and jubilation!
Dienet dem Höchsten	Serve the Most High
mit herrlichen Chören,	with magnificent choirs;
laßt uns den Namen	let us honor the name
des Herrschers verehren!	of the sovereign Lord!

As Alfred Dürr has pointed out,[1] the movements of Part I after the opening chorus can be divided into two matching halves (one presenting the perspective of Advent, the other that of Christmas), following a four-part pattern of reading, reflection, prayer, and hymn:

	Advent	Christmas
Reading:	2. Es begab sich	6. Und sie gebar
Reflection:	3. Nun wird mein liebster	7. Er ist auf Erden kommen arm
Prayer:	4. Bereite dich Zion	8. Großer Herr
Hymn:	5. Wie soll ich dich	9. Ach mein herzliebes Jesulein

Intended for Christmas Day, Part I of *The Christmas Oratorio* would have been performed in the cantata's usual liturgical position, that is, between the Gospel reading and the creed, which was followed by the sermon. Thus the narrator begins the story by quoting from the second chapter of Luke's Gospel, the reading for Christmas Day.

2. Tenor Recitative (Evangelist)

Es begab sich aber zu der Zeit, daß ein Gebot von dem Kaiser Augusto ausging, daß alle Welt geschätzet würde. Und jedermann ging, daß er sich schätzen ließe, ein jeglicher in seine Stadt. Da machte sich auch auf Joseph aus Galiläa, aus der Stadt Nazareth, in das jüdische Land zur Stadt David, die da heißet Bethlehem; darum, daß er von dem Hause und Geschlechte David war: auf daß er sich schätzen ließe mit Maria, seinem vertrauten Weibe, die war schwanger. Und als sie daselbst waren, kam die Zeit, daß sie gebären sollte.

And in those same days it came to pass that there went out a decree from Caesar Augustus, that all the world should enroll for taxes. And everyone went to be recorded, each going into his own city. Then Joseph from Galilee also went up, out of the city of Nazareth to the city of David in Judea, which is called Bethlehem, for he was of the house and lineage of David, that he might be enrolled for tax with Mary, his espoused wife, who was pregnant. And while they were there, the time came for her to give birth.

In the baroque theatrical style, recitatives, which presented the plot's development, were usually followed by arias, which reflected on the transpiring events. Here Bach departs from the traditional pattern, inserting a second (reflective) recitative. In metaphorical language borrowed from the Old Testament, the alto assumes the role of the individual believer, Christ's betrothed.

3. Alto Recitative

Nun wird mein liebster Bräutigam,
nun wird der Held aus Davids Stamm
zum Trost, zum Heil der Erden
einmal geboren werden.
Nun wird der Stern aus Jakob scheinen,
sein Strahl bricht schon hervor.
Auf, Zion,
und verlasse nun das Weinen,
dein Wohl steigt hoch empor!

Now will my beloved bridegroom,
the champion from David's line,
be born for our consolation,
for the salvation of the world.
Now will the star of Jacob shine;
its rays already break forth.
Arise, Zion,
forsake repining;
your prosperity is ascending!

In a dancelike aria the alto continues with the wedding imagery, exhorting
the betrothed (now "Zion") to prepare herself for the bridegroom. The
music, taken from the "Hercules" cantata, BWV 213, is transformed here
by means of changes in instrumentation and articulation to fit a very
different text: while the original setting ("Ich will dich nicht hören")
employed an accompaniment of unison violins marked "staccato," the
adaptation in the *Christmas Oratorio* specifies violins doubled by oboe
d'amore, and a much more lilting articulation.

4. Alto Aria (Parody of BWV 213/9)

Bereite dich, Zion,	Prepare yourself, Zion,
mit zärtlichen Trieben,	with tender emotion,
den Schönsten, den Liebsten	to greet the fairest, the dearest,
bald bei dir zu sehn!	soon in your midst!
Deine Wangen müssen heut	Your cheeks must glow
viel schöner prangen,	much fairer today;
eile, den Bräutigam	hasten to greet the bridegroom
sehnlichst zu lieben!	most ardently!

One striking feature of the *Christmas Oratorio* is the inclusion of so many
chorales (hymns). The first and last of these (Nos. 5 and 64) employ the
same tune, and thus provide an element of cyclical unity. While this tune
is now known as the "Passion Chorale" ("O Sacred Head Now
Wounded"), it did not have such an explicit association in Bach's day,
especially in Leipzig. In No. 5 the congregation responds to the alto's
foregoing exhortation with a prayer. The chorale alludes to Jesus' parable
in Matthew 25, which compares the kingdom of heaven to ten maidens
waiting for the heavenly bridegroom with oil-burning lamps. (Five of the
maidens are imprudent, and their lamps run out of oil before his arrival.)
After the chorale, the narrator continues with the story, again quoting from
the day's Gospel.

5. Chorale

Wie soll ich dich empfangen	How shall I receive you,
und wie begegn' ich dir?	and how do I approach you?
O aller Welt Verlangen,	O desire of the whole world,
o meiner Seelen Zier!	O treasure of my soul!
O Jesu, Jesu, setzte	O Jesu, Jesu, give
mir selbst die Fakkel bei,	the torch to me yourself,
damit, was dich ergötze,	so that what pleases you
mir kund	may be declared
und wissend sei!	and made known to me!

6. **Tenor Recitative** (Evangelist)

Und sie gebar ihren ersten Sohn und wikkelte ihn in Windeln und legte ihn in eine Krippen, denn sie hatten sonst keinen Raum in der Herberge.	And she gave birth to her firstborn son and wrapped him in cloths, and laid him in a manger, for there was no room for them in the inn.

After the relatively simple and straightforward narration by the Evangelist, a more complex movement occurs. Three layers of meaning can be detected. Luther's Christmas hymn, sung by the soprano(s), provides the ecclesiastical/theological perspective: Christ became poor so that the believer might be blessed with heavenly riches. A more personal view is heard from the bass singer, whose utterances are interpolated between phrases of the hymn. Above both singers are heard counter melodies played by oboe and oboe d'amore, providing reminiscences of shepherds, fields, and mangers.

7. Soprano Chorale and Bass Recitative

Er ist auf Erden kommen arm,	He came to earth poor,
Wer will die Liebe recht erhöhn, die unser Heiland für uns hegt?	Who can rightly exalt the love which our Savior bears for us?
daß er unser sich erbarm	that he might have mercy upon us
Ja, wer vermag es einzusehen, wie ihn der Menschen Leid bewegt?	Yes, who can understand how human suffering touches him?
und in dem Himmel mache reich	and make us rich in heaven,
Des höchsten Sohn kömmt in die Welt, weil ihm ihr Heil so wohl gefällt,	The Son of the Most High comes into the world because its salvation is his great desire;
und seinen lieben Engeln gleich.	and like his dear angels.
so will er selbst als Mensch geboren werden.	therefore he himself chooses to be born as man.
Kyrieleis!	Kyrieleis!

The mood changes completely with the following bass aria, in which the trumpet returns to help extol the splendor and might of the heavenly king, which have been obscured by a humble earthly birth.

8. Bass Aria (Parody of BWV 214/7)

Großer Herr, o starker König, liebster Heiland, o wie wenig achtest du der Erden Pracht! Der die ganze Welt erhält, ihre Pracht und Zier erschaffen, muß in harten Krippen schlafen.	Great Lord, O mighty King, dearest Savior, O how little you care for earthly pomp! He, who sustains the entire world, who fashioned its splendor and beauty, must sleep in a crude manger.

As is usually the pattern in Bach's cantatas, Part I of the *Christmas Oratorio* ends with a chorale. Here the subdued tone of the choir's prayer contrasts with brilliant instrumental interludes that feature the three trumpets and timpani of the very opening. Thus the music for Christmas Day comes to an end with a flourish.

9. Chorale

Ach mein herzliebes Jesulein,	Ah, little Jesus, my heart's delight,
mach dir ein rein sanft Bettelein,	make for yourself a soft little bed,
zu ruhn in meines Herzens Schrein,	to rest in my heart's shrine,
daß ich nimmer vergesse dein!	so that I never forget you!

Part II

Part II of the oratorio, intended for the second day of Christmas, begins with a sinfonia—the only purely instrumental movement in the entire work. Set in the 12/8 meter of the siciliano (a baroque dance with pastoral associations), the sinfonia sets two contrasting bodies of sound in opposition, a technique basic to the baroque concerto. On the one hand we hear the flutes and strings; on the other, the oboes d'amore and oboes da caccia (four independent parts). Perhaps Bach intended symbolic representation here: the flutes and strings exemplifying the music of the angels, the oboes symbolizing the sounds of the shepherds.

10. Sinfonia

With the orchestra having set the scene, the narrator continues the account from Luke's Gospel, describing the appearance of the angels. At this point, his story actually lags behind the story as recounted in the day's Gospel lesson. That is to say, when performed in its original liturgical setting, the Evangelist's recitative does not recapitulate the Gospel heard just moments before (as one might expect); rather, it completes the reading from the previous day. From a musical viewpoint, this recitative, like many in the *Christmas Oratorio*, is relatively straightforward. One interesting feature relates to the continuo line, which is relatively static at first, depicting the peacefulness of the pastoral scene. With the angel's appearance, however, it suddenly becomes animated, scurrying downward as the shepherds react in fear.

11. Tenor Recitative (Evangelist)
Und es waren Hirten in derselben Gegend auf dem Felde bei den Hürden, die hüteten des Nachts ihre Herde. Und siehe, des Herren Engel trat zu ihnen, und die Klarheit des Herren leuchtet um sie, und sie furchten sich sehr.

And there were shepherds in that same country, in the fields by their sheepfolds, who were keeping their flocks by night. And lo, the angel of the Lord came to them and the glory of the Lord shone round about them and they were sore afraid.

Following the narrator's account, a simple chorale affords the listeners another opportunity to internalize and appropriate the truths they have heard. This time the chorus actually takes part in the action, welcoming the angels and urging the shepherds not to react so fearfully. The instruments participate, too, doubling the vocal lines. Perhaps as a tonal allusion to the bright angel's light, Bach instructs the flutes to play the melody at the octave above.

12. Chorale
Brich an, o schönes Morgenlicht, und laß den Himmel tagen! Du Hirtenvolk, erschrekke nicht, weil dir die Engel sagen, daß dieses schwache Knäbelein soll unser Trost und Freude sein, dazu den Satan zwingen und letzlich Friede bringen!

Break forth, O beauteous morning light, and let the heavens dawn! You shepherd folk, do not be frightened, for to you the angels say, that this weak little boy child our comfort and joy shall be, and also shall Satan overpower and finally bring us peace!

The divine message of the angel (taken from the previous day's Gospel lesson) is accompanied by a "halo of strings," an effect Bach had used some years earlier in the *St. Matthew Passion* for the words of Jesus.

13. Tenor and **Soprano Recitative**
(Evangelist and Angel)
Und der Engel sprach zu ihnen: Fürchtet euch nicht, siehe, ich verkündige euch große Freude, die allem Volke widerfahren wird. Denn euch ist heute der Heiland geboren, welcher ist Christus, der Herr, in der Stadt David.

And the angel said to them, "Do not be afraid, behold, I proclaim to you joyful news, which shall be for all people. For to you there is born this day in the city of David, a Savior, who is Christ the Lord."

Another recitative follows. It explores the "shepherd relationship" between the one to whom the promise had originally come (i.e., Abraham), and those now receiving the good news from the angel. Again oboes (with their pastoral associations) are heard, punctuating the vocal lines in declamatory fashion.

14. Bass Recitative

Was Gott dem Abraham verheißen,	What God pledged to Abraham,
das läßt er nun	that he now shows the shepherd choir
dem Hirtenchor erfüllt erweisen.	as having been fulfilled.
Ein Hirt hat Alles das zuvor	A shepherd had to learn all this
von Gott erfahren müssen.	from God beforehand.
Und nun muß auch ein Hirt die Tat,	And now a shepherd must be the first
was er damals versprochen hat,	to see the deed (which he then
zuerst erfüllet wissen.	promised) accomplished.

While arias normally gave opportunity for reflection, the tenor aria (No. 15) allows the soloist to join the dramatic activity. In a movement that requires virtuosic performance from both singer and accompanying flutes, the tenor urges the shepherds to hurry as they investigate the good news. Bach's decision to accompany the singer with a flute instead of an oboe d'amore (as originally the case in Cantata 214) was apparently motivated by a desire to suggest shepherds' pipes.

15. Tenor Aria (Parody of BWV 214/5)

Frohe Hirten, eilt, ach eilet,	Happy shepherds, hasten, oh, hasten,
eh ihr euch zu lang verweilet,	lest you tarry too long.
eilt, das holde Kind zu sehn!	Hasten to see the winsome child.
Geht, die Freude heißt zu schön,	Go, the joy is just too lovely;
sucht die Anmut zu gewinnen,	seek to obtain that grace,
geht und labet Herz und Sinnen.	go and refresh heart and senses.

16. Tenor Recitative (Evangelist)

Und das habt zum Zeichen: Ihr werdet	And this will be a sign for you: you will
finden das Kind in Windeln gewickelt und	find the child wrapped in cloths and lying
in einer Krippe liegen.	in a manger.

After a brief recitative in which the Evangelist assumes the role of the angel, the chorus again joins the action. In hushed tones they encourage the shepherds to contemplate the scene described by the angel: the mystery of the manger.

17. Chorale

Schaut hin, dort liegt im finstern Stall,	Look, in yonder gloomy stable,
des Herrschaft gehet überall!	lies he whose sovereignty is over all!
Da Speise vormals sucht ein Rind,	Where once an ox sought food,
da ruhet itzt der Jungfrau'n Kind.	there rests now the virgin's child.

In No. 18 we hear the authoritative voice of a prophet, urging the shepherds to find the child. When he suggests that all join to sing a lullaby, the instruments become more animated, anticipating their involvement.

18. Bass Recitative

So geht denn hin, ihr Hirten geht,	Therefore go hence, you shepherds go,
daß ihr das Wunder seht:	that you may behold the miracle:
und findet ihr	and when you find
des Höchsten Sohn	the Son of the Most High
in einer harten Krippe liegen,	lying in a crude manger,
so singet ihm bei seiner Wiegen	then sing to him beside his cradle
aus einem süßen Ton	with a sweet tone
und mit gesamtem Chor	and with full choir
dies Lied zur Ruhe vor!	this slumber song.

But the shepherds do not leave immediately; first they rehearse the lullaby they will perform for the infant Jesus (No. 19). In accordance with the suggestion made by the bass soloist, the whole instrumental ensemble ("gesamten Chor") participates. In adapting this movement from its original setting in Cantata 213, Bach added woodwinds (oboes d'amore and da caccia double the strings, and a transverse flute doubles the voice at the upper octave), and lowered the key by a minor third. The result is a more rustic and contemplative tone. The close parallel between this text and the original one ("Schlafe, mein Liebster, und pflege der Ruh") suggests that Picander (who excelled at providing libretti for parody settings and had originally penned the "Hercules" cantata BWV 213) may have been Bach's collaborator here too.

19. Alto Aria (Parody of BWV 213/3)

Schlafe, mein Liebster, genieße der Ruh,	Sleep, my dearest, take your rest,
wache nach diesem	then keep watch afterward
vor aller Gedeihen!	over the commonweal!
Labe die Brust,	Refresh your soul,
empfinde die Lust,	experience the delight
wo wir unser Herz erfreuen!	there where our heart is gladdened!

20. Tenor Recitative (Evangelist)

Und alsobald war da bei dem Engel die	And suddenly there was with the angel,
Menge der himmlischen Heerscharen,	a multitude of the heavenly host, praising
die lobten Gott und sprachen:	God and saying:

With the appearance of the angelic host, all musical forces burst forth jubilantly, presenting the German version of the "Gloria." At the words "peace on earth" the mood changes: not only is the music now subdued in the traditional manner, but the texture is more complex—as if peace on earth is difficult to attain. At the words "good will to all men," however, jubilation breaks out again.

21. Chorus ("Evangelist")
Ehre sei Gott in der Höhe und Friede auf   Glory to God in the highest and on earth
Erden und den Menschen ein Wohl-   peace, good will to men.
gefallen.

22. Bass Recitative
So recht, ihr Engel, jauchzt und singet,   'Tis well, you angels, rejoice and sing
daß es uns heut so schön gelinget!   that we have been so fortunate today.
Auf denn! wir stimmen mit euch ein,   Arise then! We'll join with you our voices;
uns kann es so wie euch erfreun.   this brings joy to us, as it does to you.

Taking on the role of spokesperson, the bass soloist reveals his intention
to marshal all to join the hymn of praise. What follows is a more elaborate
chorale setting than heard heretofore, the instruments accompanying the
hymn in the same dancing 12/8 meter (and even some of the same
thematic material) with which Part II began.

23. Chorale
Wir singen dir in deinem Heer   Thus we sing amidst your host
aus aller Kraft   with all our might,
Lob, Preis und Ehr,   laud, praise, and honor,
daß du, o lang gewünschter Gast,   that you, O long-awaited guest
dich nunmehr eingestellet hast.   have appeared at last.

Part III

On the third (and final) day of Christmas, listeners could reasonably
expect more modest music involving smaller forces. However, Part III
begins with full festal orchestra. In several ways it recalls the celebratory
opening movement of Part I, providing a degree of cyclical unity to the
three cantatas for Christmas. This cyclical element was also present in
both of these movements' original setting: in BWV 214 (the cantata for
the birthday celebration of Electress Maria Josepha of Saxony) the music
of "Jauchzet, frohlokket" formed the first movement; the present music,
the closing movement. While the text here speaks of "feeble songs" the
music is anything but that! Bach's 96-measure structure is symmetrical:
each half begins with a purely instrumental section of sixteen measures
followed by sixteen measures of free counterpoint in which tenor, alto,
and soprano voices enter (nonimitatively) in turn, after which the instrumental section returns with voices embedded in the orchestral fabric.

24. Chorus (Parody of BWV 214/9)

Herrscher des Himmels,	Ruler of heaven,
erhöre das Lallen,	hear our faltering tones,
laß dir die matten Gesänge gefallen,	accept these feeble songs,
wenn dich dein Zion	when your Zion
mit Psalmen erhöht!	exalts you with psalms!
Höre der Herzen	Hear the jubilant
frohlokkendes Preisen,	praise of our hearts
wenn wir dir itzo	when we now manifest
die Ehrfurcht erweisen,	our reverence to you,
weil unsre Wohlfahrt befestiget steht!	for our well-being is assured.

After the exuberant choral prayer, the narrator continues his account of the Christmas story. Again his words are taken from the previous day's Gospel reading, so that cantata libretto and liturgical reading are misaligned by one day.

25. Tenor Recitative (Evangelist)

Und da die Engel von ihnen gen Himmel fuhren, sprachen die Hirten untereinander:	And as the angels rose from them toward heaven, the shepherds said to one another:

Acting the role of the shepherds, the members of the chorus begin to exhort each other to begin the search for the child in Bethlehem. In Bach's contrapuntal texture the voices run in opposite directions—some up, some down—as if no one is sure of the right road. Meanwhile the flutes scurry up and down in sixteenth notes.

26. Chorus

Lasset uns nun gehen gen Bethlehem, und die Geschichte sehen, die da geschehen ist, die uns der Herr kundgetan hat.	Let us even go now to Bethlehem and see that which has come to pass, which the Lord has made known to us.

No sooner has the choir finished than the bass soloist, taking the role of an Old Testament prophet, interjects, explaining the theological import of these events to the shepherds. Above the tones of his short speech the flutes hover like the last rays of the angels' light.

27. Bass Recitative (Voice of Old Testament prophet)

Er hat sein Volk getröst',	He has comforted his people,
er hat sein Israel erlöst,	he has redeemed his Israel,
die Hülf aus Zion hergesendet	has sent help from Zion
und unser Leid geendet.	and put an end to our suffering.
Seht, Hirten,	Behold, shepherds,
dies hat er getan;	this is what he has done;
geht, dieses trefft ihr an!	go, this is what you will find!

14

Chapter 1

The congregation realizes the prophet has been speaking to them as well, and they respond in a corporate affirmation of faith.

28. Chorale

Dies hat er alles uns getan,	All this he has done for us,
sein groß Lieb zu zeigen an;	to demonstrate his great love.
des freu sich alle Christenheit	Let all Christendom rejoice over this,
und dank ihm des in Ewigkeit.	and thank him throughout eternity for it.
Kyrieleis!	Kyrieleis!

The chorale ends with a surprisingly broad cadence—the effect is to suggest the cantata might be concluding. However a long duet for soprano and bass follows. The mood is happy, perhaps even secular. While the libretto is not, strictly speaking, a dialogue between the two voices, Bach's music resembles his love duets for soprano and bass, representing the believer and Christ, respectively. Indeed, in its original setting (the "Hercules" cantata, BWV 213) the music constitutes a love duet between the hero and virtue, complete with references to kissing and betrothal. In an apparent attempt to adapt the music to its new dramatic context (giving it a more sprightly and less sentimental mood) Bach replaced the original two violas with oboes d'amore, and raised the pitch of the movement by a major third.

29. Soprano and **Bass Duet** (Parody of BWV 213/11)

Herr, dein Mitleid, dein Erbarmen,	Lord, your compassion, your mercy,
tröstet uns und macht uns frei.	comforts us and makes us free.
Deine holde Gunst und Liebe,	Your gracious favor and love,
deine wundersamen Triebe	your wondrous propensities,
machen deine Vatertreu wieder neu.	renew your paternal faithfulness.

After the duet Bach allows the narrator to continue at some length. While Bach might have inserted an aria after the shepherds' arrival at the manger, he did not do so, preferring to highlight the words concerning Mary's introspection. As noted above, it is this very concept of "recalling former events" that marks the first part of the entire oratorio libretto.

30. Tenor Recitative (Evangelist)

Und sie kamen eilend und funden beide, Mariam und Joseph, dazu das Kind in der Krippe liegen. Da sie es aber gesehen hatten, breiteten sie das Wort aus, welches zu ihnen von diesem Kind gesaget war. Und alle, vor die es kam, wunderten sich der Rede, die ihnen die Hirten gesaget hatten. Maria aber behielt	And they hastened, and found both, Mary and Joseph, and the babe lying in a manger. And when they had seen it, they spread abroad the saying which had been told them concerning the child. And all who heard these things were filled with wonder at what the shepherds had

alle diese Worte und bewegte sie in ih-
rem Herzen.

told them. But Mary kept all these words
and pondered them in her heart.

That Bach wanted to stress Mary's moment of introspection seems clear
from the fact that the alto aria he inserted at this point is the only newly
composed aria in the entire oratorio. The lyrical duet for violin and alto
voice is perhaps the most emotionally expressive movement in the work—
one in which the Marian focus is expanded to include all individual
believers.

31. Alto Aria (Voice of Mary)

Schließe, mein Herze,
dies selige Wunder
fest in deinem Glauben ein!
Lasse dies Wunder,
die göttlichen Werke
immer zur Stärke
deines schwachen Glaubens sein!

O my heart, envelop
this blessed wonder
firmly in your faith!
Let this miracle,
the divine deeds,
ever serve to strengthen
your weak faith!

Mary's self-exhortation now yields to a statement of resolve, a recitative
accompanied by the "heavenly light" of the transverse flutes.

32. Alto Recitative (Voice of Mary)

Ja, ja, mein Herz soll es bewahren,
was es an dieser holden Zeit
zu seiner Seligkeit
für sicheren Beweis erfahren.

Yes, yes, my heart will treasure
what it has experienced
at this propitious time,
as certain proof of its salvation.

In a third contemplative response to the narrator's account, the congregation as a whole resolves to treasure not just "these words" but Jesus
himself.

33. Chorale

Ich will dich mit Fleiß bewahren,
ich will dir
leben hier,
dir will ich abfahren,
mit dir will ich endlich schweben
voller Freud
ohne Zeit
dort im andern Leben.

Diligently I'll treasure you;
I'll live
for you here,
to you I'll depart;
with you I'll soar at last,
filled with joy
unending
in that other life beyond.

In a somewhat abrupt turn, the Evangelist completes the Christmas story.
Like the other narrative movements in Part III, the text is taken from the
previous day's liturgical lesson.

34. Tenor Recitative (Evangelist)

Und die Hirten kehrten wieder um, preiseten und lobten Gott um alles, das sie gesehen und gehöret hatten, wie denn zu ihnen gesaget war.	And the shepherds returned, praising and glorifying God for all that they had seen and heard, as it had been told to them.

Following the narrator's short recitative, the choir sings one more hymn, providing further theological application for the listeners. By this point in the oratorio nine chorales have appeared, three in each cantata. Even if they were not actually sung by the congregation, their relative prevalence (even for Bach) indicates the extent to which he wanted to provide opportunity for corporate identification.

35. Chorale

Seid froh, dieweil,	Rejoice meanwhile,
daß euer Heil	that your salvation
ist hie ein Gott	has here been born,
und auch ein Mensch geboren,	God and also man;
der, welcher ist	He, who is
der Herr und Christ	the Lord and Christ,
in Davids Stadt,	in David's city,
von vielen auserkoren.	chosen from among many.

Part III ends with a repetition of its opening chorus, the instructions in the score reading, "Chorus I ab initio repetatur et claudatur."

Part IV

In Bach's day Part IV was performed on New Year's Day, whose liturgical Gospel reading conveyed the account of the circumcision and naming of Jesus. In terms of both its libretto and its musical setting this cantata is the most self-sufficient one in the oratorio. The first movement is joyful in tone (employing triple meter like the opening movements of Parts I and III), but the basic key is now F major instead of D major, and the orchestration excludes trumpets and drums. Hunting horns are featured instead, as is also the case in the "Hercules" cantata from which this movement originates. In its original setting the choral part is marked "Resolution of the Gods" (*Ratschluß der Götter*). Perhaps Bach intended the sound of the natural horns to suggest "divine pronouncement"; in the *Christmas Oratorio* one is inclined to associate it with the Hebrew shofar, one version of which was made of ibex horn (according to the Mishna), had a bell ornamented with gold, and was sounded at New Year.

36. Chorus (Parody of BWV 213/1)

Fallt mit Danken, fallt mit Loben	Fall with thanksgiving, fall with praise
vor des Höchsten Gnadenthron!	before the Most High's throne of mercy!
Gottes Sohn	God's Son
will der Erden	intends to become
Heiland und Erlöser werden,	the Savior and Redeemer of the world.
Gottes Sohn	God's Son
dämpft der Feinde Wut und Toben.	stifles the foes' rage and bluster.

Following the choral call to worship, the narrator sings the brief Gospel lesson for New Year's Day, emphasizing the name given to the infant.

37. Tenor Recitative (Evangelist)

Und da acht Tage um waren, daß das Kind beschnitten würde; da ward sein Name genennet Jesus, welcher genennet war von dem Engel, ehe denn er im Mutterleibe empfangen ward.	And when eight days were completed, so the child could be circumcised, he was named Jesus, the name given by the angel before he had been conceived in his mother's womb.

In the following recitative the bass soloist addresses Jesus in an intimate way, exploring the significance of the child's name for issues of life as well as death. Following ancient tradition the name is seen as a key to its bearer's character and significance. In the middle of the movement, in an arioso section (i.e., a section in which the rhythmic motion approaches the regularity typical of an aria), the soprano joins the bass, singing the words to a chorale's opening lines, though to a newly composed melody. To increase the prominence of the soprano melody, Bach reinforces it with the first violins.

38. Bass Recitative and **Soprano Chorale**

Immanuel, o süßes Wort!	Emmanuel, O sweet word!
Mein Jesus heißt mein Hort,	My Jesus is my refuge.
mein Jesus heißt mein Leben.	My Jesus is my life.
Mein Jesus hat sich mir ergeben,	My Jesus gave himself for me.
mein Jesus soll mir immerfort	My Jesus shall evermore
vor meinen Augen schweben.	hover before my eyes.
Mein Jesus heißet meine Lust,	My Jesus is my delight.
mein Jesus labet Herz und Brust.	My Jesus refreshes heart and breast.
Komm! Ich will dich mit Lust umfassen,	Come, I will embrace you with delight,
mein Herze soll dich nimmer lassen,	my heart shall never leave you.
ach! So nimm mich zu dir!	Ah! Then take me to yourself!
Chorale (continued in No. 40)	
Jesu, du mein liebstes Leben,	Jesus, my dearest life,
meiner Seelen Bräutigam,	bridegroom of my soul,
der du dich vor mich gegeben	you who gave yourself for me
an des bittern Kreuzes Stamm!	on the bitter cross's beam!
Auch in dem Sterben	Even in dying

sollst du mir das Allerliebste sein;	you shall be dearest of all to me;
in Not, Gefahr und Ungemach	In distress, peril, and adversity,
seh ich dir sehnlichst nach.	I look longingly after you.
Was jagte mir zuletzt	How, at the last,
der Tod für Grauen ein?	should death frighten me?
Mein Jesus! Wenn ich sterbe,	My Jesus, when I die,
so weiß ich, daß ich nicht verderbe.	I know that I shall not perish.
Dein Name steht in mir geschrieben,	Your name is graven in me;
der hat des Todes Furcht vertrieben.	it has dispelled the fear of death.

In the following echo aria (originating, like the previous movement, in Cantata 213, "Hercules at the Crossroads") the soprano soloist takes up the idea of the fear of death in relation to the name and person of Jesus. While the playful music (with its unpredictable echoes) may strike modern ears as irreverent, it must be heard within the context of the time-honored tradition in Bach's day of composing sacred dialogues. As in its original secular setting, Bach succeeds in creating an atmosphere of suspense, the text vacillating between "yes" and "no."

39. Soprano Aria (Parody of BWV 213/5)

Flößt, mein Heiland, flößt dein Namen,	My Savior, does your name
auch den allerkleinsten Samen	inspire even the smallest seed
jenes strengen Schrekkens ein?	of that severe terror?
Nein, du sagst ja selber nein!	No, you yourself say no!
Sollt ich nun das Sterben scheuen?	Should I now shy from death?
Nein, dein süßes Wort ist da!	No, your sweet word is there!
Oder sollt ich mich erfreuen?	Or should I rejoice?
Ja, du Heiland, sprichst selbst ja!	Yes, Savior, you yourself say yes!

The movement that follows parallels the earlier one for bass and soprano: the bass soloist again addresses Jesus, affirming the primacy of Jesus' name in all of life, while the soprano interjects phrases of the words to the hymn started in No. 38, though the music is again newly composed. This time, however, there is a continual alteration between recitative (bass) and arioso (soprano/bass duet) sections so that the effect is that of a love dialogue. As in the earlier companion movement, the first violins double the soprano's melody to reinforce it.

40. Bass Recitative/Arioso and **Soprano Chorale** (Continuation of chorale from No. 38)

Wohlan, dein Name soll allein	Well then, your name alone
in meinem Herzen sein!	shall dwell in my heart!
Jesu meine Freud und Wonne	Jesus, my joy and bliss,
meine Hoffnung,	my hope,
Schatz und Teil,	treasure and portion,

So will ich dich entzükket nennen,	This is what, enraptured, I shall call you,
wenn Brust und Herz	when breast and heart
zu dir vor Liebe brennen.	burn for you with love.
mein Erlösung,	my redemption,
Schmuck und Heil,	adornment and salvation,
Hirt und König,	shepherd and king,
Licht und Sonne,	light and sun;
Doch, Liebster, sage mir:	Yet, dearest, tell me:
Wie rühm ich dich,	How do I extol you,
wie dank ich dir?	thank you?
ach! wie soll ich würdiglich,	ah, how shall I worthily
mein Herr Jesu, preisen dich?	praise you, my Lord Jesus?

In a technically demanding da capo aria for tenor, two violins, and continuo, Bach employs energetic figures to depict the zealous efforts to which the poet commits himself. The sentiment parallels that of the original model (BWV 213/7), where Virtue predicts the hero's future successes. "Zealous achievement" is also an apt characterization of Bach's choice of form, for in a rare departure from his usual approach, Bach sets the solo aria as a fugue—a complex musical structure in which a distinctive musical idea is treated imitatively by all participating voices (in this case four) according to prescribed procedures. In particular, this movement demonstrates the composer's technical prowess by means of fugal devices such as theme inversion and stretto (overlapping of subject entries).

41. Tenor Aria (Parody of BWV 213/7)

Ich will nur dir zu Ehren leben,	I'll live only to your honor,
mein Heiland,	my Savior;
gib mir Kraft und Mut,	grant me strength and courage,
daß es mein Herz recht eifrig tut!	that my heart may zealously do this!
Stärke mich,	Strengthen me,
deine Gnade würdiglich	that I may worthily,
und mit Danken zu erheben!	and with gratitude, extol your grace!

Part IV of the *Christmas Oratorio* ends with an elaborate setting of a chorale text, a supplicatory prayer stressing the centrality of Jesus' name in the life of the Christian believer, a concept suited for emphasis at the beginning of a new year. The hymn's lines (whose music is probably an invention of Bach's) are embedded in a rich orchestral fabric that features concerto-like interplay between the three instrumental groups: corni da caccia, oboes, and strings.

42. Chorale

Jesus richte mein Beginnen,	Jesus, direct my commencing,
Jesus bleibe stets bei mir,	Jesus, abide ever with me,
Jesus zäume mir die Sinnen,	Jesus bridle my senses,
Jesus sei nur mein Begier,	Jesus, be my only desire.
Jesus sei mir in Gedanken,	Jesus dwell in my thoughts,
Jesu, lasse mich nicht wanken!	Jesus, let me not waver!

Part V

Part V begins with a large-scale introductory chorus of unknown origin; perhaps it was newly composed for the occasion. Concerto-like in its construction, the movement features an energetic interplay among woodwinds (two oboes d'amore), strings, and four-part chorus. Syncopated rhythms and stressed downbeats in a dancing triple meter contribute to a spirit of gaiety. Despite the complexity of the movement, its instrumentation is modest: no brass instruments or flutes are included.

43. Chorus

Ehre sei dir, Gott, gesungen,	Glory be sung to you, O God;
dir sei Lob und Dank bereit'.	praise and thanks be rendered.
Dich erhebet alle Welt,	All the world exalts you,
weil dir	because you take interest
unser Wohl gefällt,	in our well-being;
weil anheut	because this day
unser aller Wunsch gelungen,	our every wish has been granted;
weil uns dein Segen	because your blessing
so herrlich erfreut.	gladdens us so splendidly.

Written for the first Sunday after New Year, Part V takes as its narrative the liturgical lesson for the following feast day: Epiphany (January 6). As Alfred Dürr has noted, the reason probably lies in the fact that a narrative libretto requires a chronological sequence of events. Therefore the appearance of the wise men (depicted in the liturgical lesson for Epiphany) must precede Mary and Joseph's flight to Egypt (described in the reading specified for the first Sunday after New Year). In any case, just as Bach's listeners experienced misalignment between Gospel reading and cantata narration in Parts II and III, so in Part V they heard a Gospel for a different day—in this case, the liturgical reading for the following day. The story of Mary and Joseph's flight to Egypt is omitted entirely.

44. Tenor Recitative (Evangelist)

Da Jesus geboren war zu Bethlehem im jüdischen Lande zur Zeit des Königes Herodes, siehe, da kamen die Weisen vom Morgenlande gen Jerusalem und sprachen:	When Jesus was born in Bethlehem in the land of Judea, in the days of Herod the King, then wise men came from the East to Jerusalem, saying:

Introduced by the Evangelist's narration (No. 44), the chorus now assumes the role of the wise men, who have followed the star and seek the source of its light, the supposed birthplace of a new king. Bach's motet-like setting, with it rapid exchange between voices and instruments on the word "wo" ("where") suggests an eager and somewhat disorganized questioning on the part of the kingly visitors. Twice their speech is "interrupted" by the solo alto, who amplifies the biblical account (and answers the magi's question) with interpolated recitatives that provide personal theological perspectives. The oboes having fallen silent, her words are accompanied by a "halo of strings," symbolic perhaps of light.

45. Chorus and **Alto Recitative** (Magi and Christ's betrothed) (Probably adapted from BWV 247)

Wo ist der neugeborne König der Jüden?	Where is the newborn King of the Jews?
Sucht ihn in meiner Brust,	Seek him within my breast;
hier wohnt er,	here he dwells,
mir und ihm zur Lust!	to his and my delight!
Wir haben seinen Stern gesehen im Morgenlande, und sind kommen, ihn anzubeten.	We have seen his star in the East, and have come to worship him.
Wohl euch,	Blessed are you
die ihr dies Licht gesehen,	who have seen this light;
es ist	it has come to pass
zu eurem Heil geschehen!	for your salvation!
Mein Heiland, du, du bist das Licht,	My Savior, you are the light,
das auch den Heiden	which was to shine
scheinen sollen,	on the Gentiles also,
und sie,	and they,
sie kennen dich noch nicht,	though they do not yet know you,
als sie dich schon verehren wollen.	already want to worship you.
Wie hell, wie klar	How bright, how clear
muß nicht dein Schein,	must not your radiance be,
geliebter Jesu, sein!	beloved Jesus!

In the following four-part chorale, which is characterized by a marked degree of contrapuntal part-writing, the chorus takes up the theme of Epiphany (i.e., the penetration of the divine light into all the world) in a prayer for enlightenment.

46. Chorale
Dein Glanz all Finsternis verzehrt,
die trübe Nacht in Licht verkehrt.
Leit uns auf deinen Wegen,
daß dein Gesicht
und herrlichs Licht
wir ewig schauen mögen!

Your radiance consumes all darkness,
transforms the darkness into light.
Lead us in your paths,
that we may behold your face
and glorious light
eternally!

For the following aria, another prayer for moral enlightenment, Bach reused a movement from a cantata he had composed in 1734 on the occasion of a sudden visit to the Leipzig fair by the Elector of Saxony and his consort, on the anniversary of the Elector's coronation as king of Poland. Bach's ability to refit preexisting music to a new dramatic context is very much in evidence here, for he reworked the aria thoroughly. The original setting was for soprano, lay a fourth higher, had no true continuo, and included flute as well as oboe d'amore obbligato parts. To fit the music to the sentiments of the new text Bach darkened the mood by lowering the key, giving it to the deepest voice, omitting the flute, and adding continuo.

47. Bass Aria (Parody of BWV 215/7)
Erleucht auch meine finstre Sinnen,
erleuchte mein Herze
durch der Strahlen klaren Schein!
Dein Wort soll mir die hellste Kerze
in allen meinen Werken sein;
dies lässet die Seele
nichts Böses beginnen.

Illumine also my dark senses;
illumine my heart
through the rays' clear gleam!
Your word shall be for me
the brightest candle in all my deeds;
this shall avert any
evil undertaking of my soul.

The prayer for divine deliverance from the evil tendencies of human nature suddenly becomes pertinent as the Evangelist brings listeners back to the story, recounting the self-serving reaction of King Herod and his court.

48. Tenor Recitative (Evangelist)
Da das der König Herodes hörte, er-
schrak er und mit ihm das ganze Jerusa-
lem.

When King Herod heard these things, he
was alarmed, and with him all of Jerusalem.

Before the Evangelist can complete the story, the alto soloist again interjects, this time with questions intended to spur listeners to personal reflection. Her phrases are punctuated by the strings, playing trembling figures that change subtly when the subject turns to joy.

49. Alto Recitative

Warum wollt ihr erschrekken?	Why are you frightened?
Kann meines Jesu Gegenwart	Can the presence of my Jesus
euch solche Furcht erwekken?	awaken such fear in you?
O! solltet ihr euch nicht vielmehr	Oh! Should you not rather
darüber freuen,	rejoice therein,
weil er dadurch verspricht,	because he promises to restore thereby
der Menschen Wohlfahrt zu erneuen.	the well-being of mankind.

Hardly waiting for the alto to finish, the narrator continues his account of Herod's reaction. At the point where the assembled religious leaders quote an Old Testament prophecy to answer Herod's question about the predicted birthplace of the new king, Bach changes to arioso style—the melody becomes more lyrical and the overall rhythm (as especially determined by the instrumental bass) more regular.

50. Tenor Recitative (Evangelist)

Und ließ versammeln alle Hohepriester und Schriftgelehrten unter dem Volk und erforschete von ihnen, wo Christus sollte geboren werden. Und sie sagten ihm: Zu Bethlehem im jüdischen Lande; denn also stehet geschrieben durch den Propheten: Und du Bethlehem im jüdischen Lande, bist mitnichten die kleinest unter den Fürsten Juda; denn aus dir soll mir kommen der Herzog, der über mein Volk Israel ein Herr sei.	And he gathered all the high priests and the scribes of the people together, asking them where Christ should be born. And they said to him, "In Bethlehem, in the land of Judea, for thus it is written by the prophets: 'And you Bethlehem in the land of Judea are not the least of the rulers of Judah; for out of your will come forth a prince to be a ruler over my people Israel.'"

In a strikingly arranged trio, we hear a dialogue between the soprano and tenor on the one hand, and the alto (who, like Mary, has been "pondering these words in her heart") on the other. The former pair, not recognizing Christ's coming, continually ply their questions; the latter does not respond for a time, then finally enters abruptly with "Schweigt!" ("Hush!"). Above the singers a solo violin, like an unseen guest, weaves arabesques based on the motives of the soprano and tenor lines. Of the three singers it is clearly the alto who has the last word. The movement has a ternary shape, wherein a contrasting middle section sets the prayer of the last line: "Jesu, ach, so komm zu mir." Thereupon the opening material returns.

51. Soprano, Alto, and Tenor Trio

Ach, wenn wird die Zeit erscheinen,	Ah, when will the time arrive?
ach, wenn kommt	Ah, when shall the consolation
der Trost der Seinen?	of his people come?
Schweigt, er ist schon würklich hier!	Hush, he is already here!
Jesu, ach so komm zu mir!	Ah Jesus, then come to me!

In the following accompanied recitative the alto employs Johannine imagery to explain her foregoing statement: Christ reigns already in the heart of the believer.

52. Alto Recitative

Mein Liebster herrschet schon.	My beloved already reigns.
Ein Herz, das seine Herrschaft liebet,	A heart that loves his lordship,
und sich ihm ganz	and gives itself completely
zu eigen gibet,	to him to own,
ist meines Jesu Thron.	is my Jesus' throne.

Part V ends not with the royal pomp with which it began, but with the simple faith of a humble believer. In keeping with the liturgical emphasis on Epiphany it stresses the manifestation and reception of the divine light.

53. Chorale

Zwar ist solche Herzensstube	Indeed such a heart's chamber
wohl kein schöner Fürstensaal,	is indeed no beautiful royal hall,
sondern eine finstre Grube;	but rather a dark pit;
doch, sobald dein Gnadenstrahl	yet, as soon as the light of your mercy
in denselben nur wird blinken,	breaks into it,
wird es voller Sonnen dünken.	it seems full of sunshine.

Part VI

In Part VI—according to evidence gathered from surviving instrumental parts—Bach apparently reused music originating in an earlier, unidentified sacred cantata by Bach.[2] The festive orchestra, complete with three trumpets and timpani (but now without flutes), appears for the third time. Intended for performance on Epiphany, the cantata continues the narration begun in Part V. Thus the opening chorus alludes to King Herod's anger at the news of a rival king. To depict a mood of aggressive conflict, Bach chose to write an impressive fugue, whose subject is characterized by upward jabbing upward leaps. As Alfred Dürr notes, the overall ternary form is impressive in scale and design. An opening three-part orchestral ritornello of 48 measures leads into the fugue proper ("Herr, wenn die stolzen Feinde"), which is then repeated to a new set of words and instrumental doubling ("so gib, daß wir"). After a section of imitative counterpoint ("nach deiner Macht") and partial ritornello with choral material embedded ("so gib, daß wir") a contrasting middle section consisting of a canon at the fifth occurs on the final lines ("Wir wollen dir allein vertrauen"), the last part of which is accompanied by some ritornello material. A modified version of the opening material then returns. The overall structure is perfectly balanced: A (120 mm.) = B + A' (120 mm.). At times, within the busy accompaniment, "battle motives" (consisting of rapidly repeated notes) suggest the agitated style (*stile concitato*) first used in 1638 by Monteverdi in his eighth book of madrigals.

54. Chorus (Adapted from BWV 248a/1)

Herr, wenn die stolzen Feinde schnauben,	Lord, when our haughty foes rage,
so gib, daß wir im festen Glauben nach deiner Macht und Hülfe sehn!	then grant that we in firm faith look to your power and help!
Wir wollen dir allein vertrauen,	We'll place our trust in you alone;
so können wir den scharfen Klauen des Feindes unversehrt entgehn.	thus can we escape the sharp claws of the foe unharmed.

Herod's sinister plot is unveiled in the following narration.

55. Tenor and Bass Recitative (Evangelist and Herod)

Da berief Herodes die Weisen heimlich, und erlernet mit Fleiß von ihnen, wenn der Stern erschienen wäre? Und weiset sie gen Bethlehem und sprach: Ziehet hin und forschet fleißig nach dem Kindlein, und wenn ihrs findet, sagt mirs wieder, daß ich auch komme und es anbete.	Then Herod summoned the wise men secretly, and diligently ascertained of them when the star had appeared. And he sent them to Bethlehem and said, "Go there and seek the child diligently, and when you find it, bring me word, so that I also may come to worship him."

Having heard of Herod's scheming, the soprano takes it upon herself to reproach him in a dramatic, accompanied recitative.

56. Soprano Recitative (Adapted from BWV 248a/2)

Du Falscher,	Treacherous one,
suche nur den Herrn zu fällen,	just try to slay the Lord;
nimm alle falsche List,	employ all deceitful cunning
dem Heiland nachzustellen;	to waylay the Savior.
der, dessen Kraft kein Mensch ermißt, bleibt doch in sicher Hand.	He, whose power no one can measure, remains in safe hands nevertheless.
Dein Herz, dein falsches Herz ist schon, nebst aller seiner List,	Your heart, your treacherous heart, with all its cunning,

des Höchsten Sohn,	is already well known
den du zu stürzen suchst,	to the Son of the Most High,
sehr wohl bekannt.	whom you seek to destroy.

Having grown more confident and serene toward the end of her recitative, the soprano now commences a jubilant dance, celebrating the ease of a predicted victory. The music is strongly instrumental in orientation, with clear and symmetrical phrase structure, and several ritornelli sufficiently substantial and self-contained to stand alone.

57. Soprano Aria (Adapted from BWV 248a/3)

Nur ein Wink von seinen Händen	Just a wave of his hands can overthrow
stürzt ohnmächtger Menschen Macht.	the might of powerless humans.
Hier wird alle Kraft verlacht!	Here all strength is ridiculed!
Spricht der Höchste nur ein Wort,	If the Most High speaks but one word
seiner Feinde Stolz zu enden,	to put an end to the pride of his enemies,
o, so müssen sich sofort	oh, then their mortal designs
sterblicher Gedanken wenden.	are immediately be thwarted.

The narrator now turns the listener's attention back to the story.

58. Tenor Recitative (Evangelist)

Als sie nun den König gehöret hatten,	Now when they had heard the king, they
zogen sie hin. Und siehe, der Stern, den	departed. And lo, the star that they had
sie im Morgenlande gesehen hatten,	seen in the east went before them until it
ging für ihnen hin, bis daß er kam, und	came and stood over where the young
stund oben über, da das Kindlein war.	child was. When they saw the star they
Da sie den Stern sahen, wurden sie	rejoiced greatly and went into the house
hoch erfreuet und gingen in das Haus	and found the young child with Mary his
und funden das Kindlein mit Maria, sei-	mother, and they fell down and wor-
ner Mutter, und fielen nieder und beteten	shiped him and opened their treasures
es an und täten ihre Schätze auf und	and gave to him gold, frankincense, and
schenkten ihm Gold, Weihrauch und	myrrh.
Myrrhen.	

With the wise men having found the house where Jesus was and given their gifts in worship, the congregation responds in kind. In a bit of traditional poetic licence they imagine themselves (and the wise men) at the manger, where they offer their very selves to the Christ child.

59. Chorale

Ich steh an deiner Krippen hier,	I stand by your manger here,
o Jesulein, mein Leben;	O Jesus child, my life;
ich komme, bring und schenke dir,	I come, bring, and give to you,
was du mir hast gegeben.	what you have given me.
Nimm hin!	Take it!
es ist mein Geist und Sinn,	It is my spirit and disposition,

Herz, Seel und Mut,	heart, soul, and mettle;
nimm alles hin,	take it all,
und laß dirs wohl gefallen!	and may it please you well!

With the following recitative the Evangelist brings the Epiphany account to an end. The magi are warned about Herod's intentions and they escape by a different route. Bach's musical setting is relatively simple at first: a ten-beat pedal tone undergirds the singer's line for the opening measures (as is often the case in Bach's recitatives). For the final cadence, however, the harmonies take a strikingly circuitous route at the words "they went back by another way."

60. Tenor Recitative (Evangelist)

Und Gott befahl ihnen im Traum, daß sie	And God commanded them in a dream
sich nicht sollten wieder zu Herodes	not to return to Herod, and they went
lenken, und zogen durch einen andern	back by another way into their own land.
Weg wieder in ihr Land.	

Reflecting on the wise men's departure, the tenor sings a recitative accompanied by two oboes d'amore, which play frequent sighing figures.

61. Tenor Recitative (Adapted from BWV 248a/4)

So geht!	Begone then!
Genug, mein Schatz geht nicht von hier,	Enough! My treasure will not leave,
er bleibet da bei mir,	he will stay by me;
ich will ihn auch nicht von mir lassen.	I'll also not let him part from me.
Sein Arm wird mich aus Lieb	His arm will embrace me in love,
mit sanftmutsvollem Trieb	with gentle desire
und größter Zärtlichkeit umfassen;	and the greatest tenderness.
er soll mein Bräutigam verbleiben,	He shall remain my bridegroom;
ich will ihm Brust und Herz	I'll ascribe breast and heart
verschreiben.	to him.
Ich weiß gewiß, er liebet mich,	I am certain that he loves me;
mein Herz liebt ihn auch inniglich	my heart also loves him fervently
und wird ihn ewig ehren.	and will ever revere him.
Was könnte mich nun für ein Feind	What foe could hurt me now
bei solchem Glück versehren!	amidst such prosperity!
Du, Jesu,	You, Jesus,
bist und bleibst mein Freund;	are and will remain my friend;
und werd ich ängstlich zu dir flehn:	and if I implore you anxiously,
Herr, hilf!, so laß mich Hülfe sehn!	"Lord, help!" then let me see your aid!

The two oboes d'amore continue to accompany the tenor in the aria that follows. In its textual emphasis the movement relates to the opening chorus (in vain the foe rages against the Christ child and his followers), and Bach's setting has a correspondingly strong forward drive. The instruments provide interludes, and they respond in concerto-like fashion to the vocal motives. Three times, however, the vigorous rhythm is unexpectedly halted. The dramatic reason appears to be the singer's wandering attention: as he ponders his mystic love relationship with Jesus ("mein Schatz . . . ist hier bei mir") he momentarily forgets his aggressive posture.

62. Tenor Aria (Adapted from BWV 248a/5)

Nun mögt ihr stolzen Feinde schrekken;	Now you proud foes can try to terrify;
was könnt ihr mir	what fear
für Furcht erwekken?	can you arouse in me?
Mein Schatz, mein Hort ist hier bei mir.	My treasure, my refuge is here with me.
Ihr mögt euch noch so grimmig stellen,	You may appear ever so fierce,
droht nur, mich ganz und gar zu fällen,	threaten to bring me down completely,
doch seht! mein Heiland wohnet hier.	yet see, my Savior dwells here!

A brief triumphant exchange amongst the four solo voices (with a fanfare-like motive carried imitatively from one to the another) ensues. Each successive vocal entry introduces a new key. The resulting sense of tonal instability eases at the end, and the music comes to rest in D major.

63. S. A. T. B. Recitative (Adapted from BWV 248a/6)

Was will der Hölle Schrekken nun,	What can hell's terror now do,
was will uns Welt und Sünde tun,	what can world and sin do,
da wir in Jesu Händen ruhn?	since we rest in Jesus' hands?

Bach ends the oratorio with an elaborate chorale arrangement for full orchestra and chorus. The impressive instrumental opening, featuring a variation of the fanfare motive heard in the previous recitative, already suggests that this movement will exceed all previous ones in splendor, but gives no hint of the chorale to be included. Indeed the structure of the movement is essentially that of an instrumental concerto (characterized by interplay amongst the various instrument groups) into which the phrases of the hymn, harmonized in four-parts, are intermittently embedded. Bach's skill at combining disparate musical elements is evidenced by the fact that he reconciles the "tonality" of the chorale (Phrygian on F♯) with the key of the movement as a whole (the festal key of D major). Through-out the movement the first trumpet plays a prominent role, leading the victory celebration, as it were, and helping to bring the Christmas story to a triumphant close.

64. Chorus (Chorale) (Adapted from
BWV 248a/7)

Nun seid ihr wohl gerochen	Now you are well avenged
an eurer Feinde Schar,	against your horde of foes,
denn Christus hat zerbrochen,	for Christ has broken
was euch zuwider war.	what was opposing you.
Tod, Teufel, Sünd und Hölle	Death, devil, sin, and hell
sind ganz und gar geschwächt;	are completely weakened;
bei Gott hat seine Stelle	the human race
das menschliche Geschlecht.	has its place with God.

Notes

1. Alfred Dürr, *Die Kantaten von Johann Sebastian Bach mit ihren Texten*, 2 vols. (Kassel: Bärenreiter, 1985), 1:133.

2. Dürr, *Die Kantaten*, 1:215.

2
St. John Passion (BWV 245)

B ach's Passions mark the culmination of a centuries-long history of Passion music. As early as the medieval period, the Passion story was read (chanted) in a semi-dramatic fashion, using three different ranges of the voice for the roles of the story: the part of Jesus was sung in low range, that of the narrator (Evangelist) in mid-range, and that of the crowd (*turba*) in high range. By the mid-1200s the roles of the Passion were distributed among several individuals for more realistic effect. Still later, composers began incorporating polyphony in their compositions—usually for the words of the crowd but occasionally also for the utterances of other characters. Such settings were intended to help re-create for the listener a first-hand experience of the story.

In the early sixteenth century (after the Reformation of 1517) Passions in Protestant Germany were sometimes monophonic (i.e., they consisted of unaccompanied, single strands of melody), sometimes polyphonic (multiple simultaneous melodic lines), or, at times, a mixture of the two (the narrative parts sung as monophony, individual character parts as polyphony). Passions could also be in either Latin or German.

After 1650 the trend toward ever more emotive texts led to the appearance of the oratorio Passion in northern Germany. This type retained the biblical text for the main characters (Evangelist, Jesus, Pilate, crowd, etc.), and expanded it with poetic texts of a reflective nature, sinfonias, other biblical texts, newly created poetry, and chorales (hymns). As to their form, oratorio Passions more or less resembled operas—that is, the soloists presented recitatives (narratives sung in a manner that approximates speech) and arias (song-like movements in which melodic considerations are primary, the action stops, and the character reflects on what has transpired). Unlike operas, however, oratorio Passions were not staged. The earliest oratorio Passions appeared in Hamburg, which was an important operatic center in Germany.

By the 1700s there were four basic types of sung Passions: the simple old type (no instruments, some embellishment of the story with hymns), the oratorio Passion (biblical text with insertions as described above), the Passion oratorio (completely original text; i.e., no Bible text), and the lyrical Passion meditation (no direct dialogue).[1]

Bach's obituary reported that he had written five Passions. In fact, there were probably only four since the *St. Luke Passion* is not authentic. Of the remaining ones, unfortunately only the *St. John* and the *St. Matthew* survive intact. The *St. Mark* was destroyed in World War II (although the text survives). A fourth one was perhaps a *St. Matthew Passion* from the end of Bach's stay in Weimar, written for a 1717 performance in Gotha. Recent research suggests that some of the music in the *St. John* and *St. Matthew* were taken from this work.

Both of Bach's extant Passions are oratorio Passions. This type was important to orthodox Lutherans because its libretto adhered closely to a single Gospel text. However, when Bach came to Leipzig the oratorio Passion was a relatively new phenomenon. Leipzig was a conservative city and resisted overly theatrical music in church. In fact, when Bach's *St. John Passion* was premiered in 1724, oratorio Passions had been heard in Leipzig's principal churches in only three previous years. Martin Geck writes:

> Leipzig audiences had little experience of large-scale oratorio Passions scored for elaborate forces. In 1717 one of Telemann's Passions had been performed in the *Neukirche* (something of a sideshow on the city's musical scene), and in 1721 and 1722 Bach's predecessor, Johann Kuhnau, had made a modest and somewhat halfhearted attempt to perform a concert Passion. In this respect, there was no comparison with Hamburg, where the Passion oratorio had become something of an institution in the city's musical life—not, of course, as part of the divine service but within the framework of concert performances. As early as 1705 Hamburg's concert-goers had been able to hear a setting of Christian Friedrich Hunold's oratorio *Der blutige und sterbende Jesus* by the director of the Hamburg opera, Reinhard Keiser, in a performance for which admission was charged and which took the form of a theatrical production "on a stage specially prepared for the occasion" at the city's almshouse. . . . In Leipzig the influence of traditional theology and religion was far greater, with the result that the sort of conditions that obtained in Hamburg were altogether unthinkable: it is no accident

that, on taking up his appointment, Bach had to agree not to write in an excessively operatic vein. . . . Not that the new Thomaskantor harbored any such thoughts. Far from it. Even at this early stage . . . the great universalist was already striving to merge the old with the new, the sacred with the secular, the functional with the autonomous, general sublimity with individual beauty. His music can be read as a perfect reflection of an age that knows a yesterday, a today and a tomorrow.[2]

Bach's *St. John Passion* was first performed at the afternoon Vespers Service on Good Friday, April 7, 1724, the composer's first Easter in that city. It is possible that he had written the work in the months preceding the move, in anticipation of his new position. On the other hand, if he wrote it after assuming the position with its associated hectic schedule, he probably did so during Lent when cantatas were generally not required (an exception was the Feast of the Annunciation—March 25).

There is little question that Bach intended the *St. John Passion* to have great dramatic force. The narrative is taut: the action is fast-paced, and dramatic contrasts are starkly drawn (e.g., the depiction of a divine, serene Jesus over against a bloodthirsty, howling mob). Bach clearly expected the biblical narration itself to provide much of the work's emotional impact, for he gave to the Evangelist a particularly demanding and often highly expressive part (cf. the passage depicting Peter's tearful remorse).

Polyphonic music was forbidden in Leipzig during the final weeks of Advent and during Lent, although the first Sunday of Advent and the Feast of the Annunciation were exceptions to this rule. Imagine what it must have been like to hear a work such as the *St. John Passion* after a "tempus clausum" with nothing but simple hymns and chants!

Passions were traditionally performed on Good Friday in the afternoon (Vespers) service. The liturgy for that day was essentially a simplified version of Sunday Vespers. The first part of the Passion came before the sermon (replacing the cantata of a normal Sunday); the second part followed the sermon (replacing the usual *Magnificat*). The order of service was:[3]

Hymn ("Da Jesus an dem Kreuze stund")
Passion, Part I
Sermon
Passion, Part II
Motet: "Ecce quomodo moritur" by Jacob Handl (1550–91)
Collect
Benediction
Hymn: "Nun danket alle Gott"

Since only two of Bach's Passions survive, it is illuminating to compare them. In general the *St. John* is more realistic, faster paced, and more anguished than the reflective and resigned *St. Matthew*. It is shorter and less episodic, with fewer reflective interpolations. It also has simpler orchestration than the *St. Matthew*, which calls for double choir and orchestra.

> While Bach rendered St. Matthew's Gospel on a grand scale . . . his treatment of St. John's narrative, with its focus on the lengthy argument between Pilate and the [religious leaders] over Jesus' fate, is more intensely dramatic. At the same time, its simplicity and smaller scale make it a very intimate, personal work.[4]

In the monumental and expansive *St. Matthew*, a series of short scenes are interrupted by frequent lyrical meditations provided by soloists or vocal ensemble, giving the entire work a contemplative tone. The *St. John* keeps its focus on the story itself—the rapidly unfolding events of a great travesty of justice, which must nevertheless be understood as the predestined plan of a sovereign God. That the overall shape and tone of the *St. John* were determined in part by the nature of the Johannine account itself has been noted by Andreas Glöckner, who writes:

> Bach's decision to set to music the unabridged Passion story according to St. John had serious consequences for the conception of the work as a whole, since in only a few places . . . did it allow the insertion of reflective arias and ariosos, and even after revising the work several times Bach arrived at no completely satisfactory solution to the problem of just where to position these sections of contemplative commentary. . . . Two musically especially rewarding sections, where Peter weeps and where the veil of the temple is torn apart, are borrowed from the St. Matthew Gospel. . . . Bach lends them weight by means of motivic development in metrically anchored recitative, and inserts lengthy contemplative sections into them.[5]

It has been said that the *St. John Passion* lacks textual unity. The reason for this is that "the text is something of a mongrel."[6] It may well have been compiled by the composer himself, "choosing texts from existing Passion poems and altering them, if necessary, to fit his concept."[7] While most of the biblical text is from the Gospel of John, there are also some passages from the Gospel of Matthew: Peter's remorse and the earthquake scene. The nonbiblical material comes from several sources: mostly from a famous devotional Passion poem by B. H. Brockes, *Der für die Sünde der*

Welt gemarterte und sterbende Jesus (1712) (which had been set by other composers, including Handel and Telemann) and the *St. John Passion* libretto by C. H. Postel (c. 1700).

Bach revised the work several times. Unlike the *St. Matthew*, the *St. John Passion* existed in several versions—at least four. In version II (1725—the year Bach composed many chorale cantatas) he replaced or augmented several movements. The opening chorus, "Herr, unser Herrscher," was displaced by a chorale fantasia, "O Mensch bewein' dein Sünde groß," and the closing chorale, "Ach Herr, laß dein lieb Engelein," by a lengthy chorale setting of "Christe, du Lamm Gottes" from Cantata 23. In Version III (c. 1732), he removed the substitute numbers (for example, now that "O Mensch bewein' dein Sünde groß" had been incorporated in the *St. Matthew*, he removed it from the *St. John* and replaced it with the original opening movement, "Herr, unser Herrscher"), removed the interpolations from the Gospel of Matthew, and made some other changes. In the fourth and final version (1749) Bach restored the deleted movements, largely reestablishing the original sequence (which now again included the interpolations from the Gospel of Matthew), and enriched the orchestration.[8]

The final result is a work of great dramatic force. Much of this is due to the intensity of the Evangelist's part, which is extremely demanding. While the *St. Matthew Passion* presents Christ as the divine sufferer (thus, for example, Bach always accompanies the sung words of Jesus with strings, a kind of "halo" effect), the *St. John* presents Christ's suffering in all its human agony. This may have been the reason for Bach's decision *not* to orchestrate the words of Jesus, even in the later versions, despite his familiarity with this practice (earlier in his career he had arranged Reinhard Keiser's Passion, which accompanies Jesus' words with strings) and his later adoption of the practice in the *St. Matthew Passion*. In one sense this emphasis on Jesus' humanity is surprising, for the Gospel of John stresses Christ's divinity more emphatically than the other three Gospels. Nevertheless, because John's Gospel also provides more detail concerning the trial before Pilate, the story becomes more gripping in human terms. Thus Bach's *St. John Passion* became more impassioned than the later *St. Matthew*.

A special feature of Bach's two Passions is the frequent appearance of chorales. Both Passions incorporate more chorales than was usual at the time: thirteen in the *St. Matthew*, eleven in the *St. John*. Although these hymns were probably sung without congregational participation they nevertheless represent the corporate response of the faithful, and their frequency suggests a desire on Bach's part to elicit a response from his listeners throughout the unfolding of the story.

In the *St. John Passion* the chorales sometimes incorporate dramatic action. Thus, for example, in the chorale "Petrus, der nicht denkt zurrück" (No. 14 [20]) the choir comments on Peter's denial of Christ. While these hymn tunes would have been familiar to Bach's audience, his harmonizations were new and often exceptionally rich, highlighting the significance of particular words or phrases. Marion Metcalf writes:

> Because the words and tunes were familiar to seventeenth-century Lutherans (many had been used since Luther's time), the chorales provided the work's most direct linkage between the story and the religious responses of the devout listener. Bach's settings of the chorales masterfully reinforce their meaning.[9]

Sometimes Bach uses a chorale as the basis for an elaborate musical setting. Part I of the *St. John Passion*, for example, opens and closes with chorale-based movements. In such movements the hymn provides an additional layer of musical and textual meaning.

A significant formal characteristic of the *St. John Passion* is its symmetry, which is especially evident in the group of movements that culminate with Jesus' crucifixion. Audrey Wong and Norm Proctor write:

> The work is flanked by two massive choruses, the opening "Herr, unser Herrscher," a complex and compelling invocation, and the ending "Ruht wohl," a sweet and lingering grave side parting. Within this framework Bach transcends mere sequence of individual numbers by arranging musically similar choruses symmetrically around a central chorale. Nine choral movements, the last four mirroring the first four, revolve around the pivot point in the drama, the height of the psycho-emotional conflict, when Pilate searches for a way to release Christ while the high priests scream for Christ to die.

> Here and throughout the work, Bach pairs off choral movements that share similar texts or sentiments. The music with which the soldiers mockingly hail the King of the Jews reappears when the priests demand that Pilate "write not that he is King of the Jews." A more ironic pairing is Bach's choice of the same chorale tune to contemplate first Peter's thoughtlessly denying his master and then Jesus's thoughtfully providing for his mother.[10]

More details about this aspect of the work appear below, in the introduction to Part II of the work.

One of the criticisms leveled against the *St. John Passion* in recent years is its apparent anti-Jewish sentiments. The symmetry produced by the "terrifying repetitions" of "Crucify, crucify!" and the text's repeated negative references to the "Jews," could lead one to that conclusion. But as Michael Marissen points out in his book, *Lutheranism, Anti-Judaism, and Bach's St. John Passion*[11] Bach made numerous compositional choices that suggest Bach intended no such interpretation. More fundamentally, the libretto, generally reflecting Lutheran theology of Bach's day, lays the blame for Jesus' death on all of humanity, and presents the cross as divine victory.

Part I

(Note: For the convenience of readers using music scores employing the older numbering system rather than the one used in the new collected edition, movement numbers are given according to both schemes whenever they differ.)[12]

Part I of the *St. John Passion* encompasses Jesus' betrayal, his appearance before the high priest, Caiaphas, and Peter's remorse after his denial of Christ. The opening chorus is a magnificent da capo movement in G minor, whose text begins with an allusion to Psalm 8: "O Lord, how majestic is your name in all the earth!" Despite the positive sentiment of the opening words, the mood is ominous. A static bass line pulses relentlessly while the violins play buzzing circular figures of sixteenth notes and the woodwinds play harmonic suspensions in longer note values. After a buildup of eighteen measures the choir enters with a threefold cry of "Herr" ("Lord"), reminiscent of the "Sanctus" calls of the seraphim in Isaiah 6:3, then take up the circular sixteenth-note figure with the strings. An imitative section for the voices follows at measure 33. Here the instrumental roles are reversed: the bass instruments now play the circular figure, while the strings interject jabbing eighth notes. Then follow the words that are key to understanding a central theme of this Passion setting: "Show us through your Passion that you, the true Son of God, at all times, even in the greatest abasement, have been glorified." The idea that Christ's crucifixion was also his glorification is a central concept in this work. Historically, it relates to Luther's theology of the cross. Many of Bach's compositions reflect it. The idea also explains an apparent contradiction: while John's Gospel (more than any of the other Gospels) emphasizes Jesus' divinity, its portrayal of the trial and death of Jesus (and thus also Bach's *St. John Passion*) is vividly human.

The entire B section of the opening chorus is a marvel of harmonic tension, which finally finds resolution in D major. Thereupon the opening section in G minor returns.

1. Chorus

Herr, unser Herrscher,	Lord, our sovereign,
dessen Ruhm	whose renown
in allen Landen herrlich ist!	is glorious in all lands!
Zeig uns durch deine Passion,	Show us by your Passion
daß du, der wahre Gottessohn,	that you, the true Son of God,
zu aller Zeit,	were glorified
auch in der größten Niedrigkeit,	at all times,
verherrlicht worden bist.	even in the greatest abasement.

As the narrator begins his account the listener is immediately submersed in human conflict: the inflamed rabble, led by the treacherous Judas, comes to arrest Jesus, who responds with surprising composure.

2a. (2.) Recitative (Evangelist and Jesus)

Jesus ging mit seinen Jüngern über den Bach Kidron, da war ein Garte, darein ging Jesus und seine Jünger. Judas, aber, der ihn verriet, wußte den Ort auch, denn Jesus versammelte sich oft daselbst mit seinen Jüngern. Da nun Judas zu sich hatte genommen die Schar und der Hohenpriester und Pharisäer Diener, kommt er dahin mit Fakkeln, Lampen und mit Waffen. Als nun Jesus wußte alles, was ihm begegnen sollte, ging er hinaus und sprach zu ihnen: Wen suchet ihr? Sie antworten ihm:

Jesus went with his disciples over the brook Kidron: a garden was there, which Jesus entered and his disciples. But Judas, who betrayed him, knew the place also, for Jesus and his disciples often gathered there. When Judas had assembled around him the cohort and the servants of the high priests and Pharisees, he came there with torches, lanterns, and with weapons. Then when Jesus knew all things that were to come upon him, he went out and said to them, "Whom do you seek?" They answered him:

The crowd, apparently not recognizing Jesus, answers with a threefold repetition of Jesus' name, mirroring the "Lord, Lord, Lord" of the opening chorus. With the Oboe I acting as stimulus, the crowd retorts with menacingly abrupt jabs. The melodic movement drives toward the word "Nazareth," as if to emphasize the stigma of coming from such a lowly town, perhaps alluding to the proverb "Can anything good come from Nazareth?" (John 1:46) The movement is short and fast-paced, and the action continues without pause.

2b. (3.) Chorus

Jesum von Nazareth.   Jesus of Nazareth.

2c. (4.) Recitative (Evangelist and Jesus)

Jesus spricht zu ihnen: Ich bins. Judas aber, der ihn verriet, stund auch bei ihnen. Als nun Jesus zu ihnen sprach: Ich bins, wichen sie zurükke und fielen zu Boden. Da fragete er sie abermal: Wen suchet ihr? Sie aber sprachen:

Jesus said to them, "I am the one." But Judas, who betrayed him, also stood there among them. Now when Jesus said to them, "I am the one!" they shrank backward and fell to the ground. Then he asked them a second time, "Whom do you seek?" They answered:

When Jesus repeats his question, the mob answers as before, whereupon Jesus argues for the release of the other hostages.

2d. (5.) Chorus

Jesum von Nazareth.

Jesus of Nazareth.

2e. (6.) Recitative (Evangelist and Jesus)

Jesus antwortete: Ich habs euch gesagt, daß ichs sei, suchet ihr denn mich, so lasset diese gehen!

Jesus answered, "I have told you that I am he; if you are seeking me, then let these go!"

Jesus' concern for others over himself is observed wonderingly by the chorus and internalized. The hymn interpolated here is, in a sense, an interruption of the narrator's thought. While the mood is serious—even lamenting—the chorale ends with the brightness of a major chord, suggesting that the ultimate effect of these events will be positive.

3. (7.) Chorale

O große Lieb,
O Lieb ohn alle Maße,
die dich gebracht
auf these Marterstraße!
Ich lebte mit der Welt
in Lust und Freuden,
und du mußt leiden.

O great love,
O love without measure,
which brought you
upon this martyr's road!
I lived with the world
in pleasure and joy,
and you must suffer.

While Jesus concerns himself with the safety of his disciples, Peter tries to defend him. But Jesus rejects his help, heals the injured enemy, and declares that these events have been allowed by God the Father.

4. (8.) Recitative (Evangelist and Jesus)

Auf daß das Wort erfüllet würde, welches er sagte: Ich habe der keine verloren, die du mir gegeben hast. Da hatte Simon Petrus ein Schwert und zog es aus und schlug nach des Hohenpriesters Knecht und hieb ihm sein recht Ohr ab; und der

So that the word might be fulfilled which he had spoken, "I have not lost one of those whom you have given me." Then Simon Peter, having a sword, drew it and struck at the high priest's servant, and cut off his right ear; and the servant was

Knecht hieß Malchus. Da sprach Jesus	named Malchus. Then Jesus said to
zu Petro: Stekke dein Schwert in die	Peter, "Put your sword in its scabbard.
Scheide! Soll ich den Kelch nicht trinken,	Shall I not drink the cup that my Father
den mir mein Vater gegeben hat?	has given me?"

In contrast to the impulsive actions of Peter, the chorus commits itself to yielding to the unfathomable will of God. In the original Bach source, only the first phrase of the text is given, suggesting that the hymn was familiar enough to be rendered by memory.

5. (9.) Chorale

Dein Will gescheh, Herr Gott,	Your will be done, Lord God,
zugleich auf Erden	on earth
wie im Himmelreich.	as it is done in heaven.
Gib uns Geduld in Leidenszeit,	Give us patience in time of suffering,
gehorsam sein in Lieb und Leid;	obedience in weal and woe;
wehr und steur	restrain and steer
allem Fleisch und Blut,	all flesh and blood
Das wider deinen Willen tut!	that works against your will!

After Jesus is bound and brought before the religious officials, the high priest ironically utters a theologically profound statement: it would be better that one man perished than a whole nation.

6. (10.) Recitative (Evangelist)

Die Schar aber und der Oberhauptmann	But the cohort and the captain, and the
und die Diener der Jüden nahmen	servants of the Jews took Jesus and
Jesum und bunden ihn und führeten ihn	bound him, and led him away at first to
aufs erste zu Hannas, der war Kaiphas	Annas, the father-in-law of Caiaphas,
Schwäher, welcher des Jahres Hoher-	who was high priest that year. Now it
priester war. Es war aber Kaiphas, der	was this same Caiaphas who counseled
den Juden riet, es wäre gut, daß ein	that it would be well that one man perish
Mensch würde umbracht für das Volk.	for the people.

With an accompaniment of imitatively intertwining oboes and an instrumental bass that doubles back on itself (both of which probably suggest the binding of Jesus' hands), the alto presents the first aria of the Passion—a da capo aria of great pathos in which the paradoxically beneficial effects of the transpiring events are considered.

7. (11.) Alto Aria

Von den Strikken meiner Sünden	From the bands of my sins,
mich zu entbinden,	to unbind me,
wird mein Heil gebunden.	is my Salvation bound.
Mich von allen Lasterbeulen	From all my iniquitous boils
völlig zu heilen,	fully to heal me,
läßt er sich verwunden.	he lets himself be wounded.

8. (12.) Recitative (Evangelist)

Simon Petrus aber folgete Jesu nach und ein ander Jünger.	But Simon Peter followed Jesus, and another disciple.

After we are told that Peter is still following his master, we are treated to a dance-like aria in which the soprano addresses Jesus directly, affirming a commitment to follow him with joy. Set in triple meter (whose effect is heightened by a bass often playing off-beats only) with an accompaniment of flutes, the aria provides welcome relief from the tension of the preceding movements. Because the lines imitate each other, "'Ich folge dir gleichfalls' can be interpreted as a lively, if strictly imitative, passepied [a baroque dance] but also as a literal illustration of the idea of *imitatio Christi*."[13]

9. (13.) Soprano Aria

Ich folge dir gleichfalls	I follow you likewise
mit freudigen Schritten,	with joyful footsteps,
und lasse dich nicht,	and will not leave you,
mein Leben, mein Licht.	my life, my light.
Befördre den Lauf	Assist my course,
und höre nicht auf	and do not cease
selbst an mir zu ziehen,	to draw me,
zu schieben, zu bitten.	to spur me, to call me.

A long dramatic narration, in which Jesus, Peter, a maid, and a servant sing their respective roles, describes the first interrogation by the religious officials. Peter's cowardly denial of knowing Jesus is contrasted with Jesus' majestic words, "I have taught openly before the world . . . and have said nothing in secret. Why do you ask me? Ask those who heard me!" A shivering Peter, meanwhile, still wanting to stay near his master, warms himself at the fire in the courtyard with the others. An interesting example of Bach's rhetorical mastery occurs at the text "The officers and the servants had made a fire of coals, for it was cold, and were standing and warming themselves," where the narrator's voice first rises abruptly for "cold' and then shivers on the word "warming."

10. (14.) Recitative (Evangelist, Maid, Peter, Jesus, and Servant)

Derselbige Jünger war dem Hohen-priester bekannt und ging mit Jesu hinein in des Hohenpriesters Palast. Petrus aber stund draußen vor der Tür. Da ging der andere Jünger, der dem Hohen-priester bekannt war, hinaus, und redete mit der Türhüterin und führete Petrum hinein. Da sprach die Magd, die Tür-	That disciple was known to the high priest, and he went with Jesus into the high priest's palace. But Peter stood outside at the door. Then the other disci-ple, who was known to the high priest, went out and spoke to the girl that watched the door, and brought Peter inside. Then the maid watching the door

hüterin, zu Petro: Bist du nicht dieses Menschen Jünger einer? Er sprach: Ich bins nicht. Es stunden aber die Knechte und Diener und hatten ein Kohlfeu'r gemacht (denn es war kalt), und wärmeten sich. Petrus aber stund bei ihnen und wärmete sich.

said to Peter, "Are you not one of this person's disciples?" He said, "I am not." But the officers and the servants had made a fire of coals, for it was cold, and were standing and warming themselves. Peter also stood among them and warmed himself.

Aber der Hohenpriester fragte Jesum um seine Jünger und um seine Lehre. Jesus antwortete ihm: Ich habe frei, öffentlich geredet vor der Welt. Ich habe allezeit gelehret in der Schule und in dem Tempel, da alle Juden zusammenkommen, und habe nichts im Verborgnen geredt. Was fragest du mich darum? Frage die darum, die gehöret haben, was ich zu ihnen geredet habe! Siehe, dieselbigen wissen, was ich gesaget habe. Als er aber solches redete, gab der Diener einer, die dabeistunden, Jesu einen Bakkenstreich und sprach: Solltest du dem Hohenpriester also antworten? Jesus aber antwortete: Hab ich übel geredt, so beweise es, daß es böse sei; hab ich aber recht geredt, was schlägest du mich?

But the high priest asked Jesus about his disciples and his teaching. Jesus answered, "I have spoken openly before the world. I have taught constantly in the school and in the temple, where all the Jews come together, and have said nothing in secret. Why do you ask me? Ask those who heard me about what I said to them. Look, they know what I said!" But when he said these things one of the servants who stood nearby struck him in the face and said, "Should you answer the high priest this way?" But Jesus said, "If I have spoken wickedly, prove it; but if I have spoken correctly, why do you strike me?"

The chorus immediately internalizes the action, concluding that the blame lies ultimately not with these religious leaders but with the sins of all humanity.

11. (15.) Chorale

Wer hat dich so geschlagen,
mein Heil, und dich mit Plagen
so übel zugericht'?
Du bist ja nicht ein Sünder,
wie wir und unsre Kinder,
von Missetaten weißt du nicht.

Who struck you in this way,
my Salvation; and with torment
treated you so badly?
For you are no sinner
like us and our children;
you know nothing of evildoing.

Ich, ich und meine Sünden,
die sich wie Körnlein finden
des Sandes an dem Meer,
die haben dir erreget
das Elend, das dich schläget,
und das betrübte Marterheer.

I, I and my sins,
which are as many as the grains
of sand on the seashore,
they have brought you
the misery that has struck you,
and the miserable band of torturers.

After Jesus is sent away for further interrogation, Peter faces his second test. This time he is confronted by several bystanders who hound him with their accusations.

12a. (16.) Recitative (Evangelist)

Und Hannas sandte ihn gebunden zu dem Hohenpriester Kaiphas. Simon Petrus stund und wärmete sich; da sprachen sie zu ihm:

Now Annas sent Jesus bound to the high priest Caiaphas. Simon Peter stood and warmed himself. Then they said to him:

Bach's setting is brilliant: the hissing questions come ever quicker, nipping at the beleaguered Peter from all directions.

12b. (17.) Chorus

Bist du nicht seiner Jünger einer?

Are you not one of his disciples?

When Peter denies Christ a third time the cock crows, and he suddenly remembers Jesus' warning. Realizing what he has done, he collapses in remorse. The scene is one of the most memorable moments in the work. While the Evangelist's narration to this point has been expressive but straightforward, it now abandons all objectivity—the highly chromatic line for the text "und weinete bitterlich" (all twelve chromatic tones are included in the vocal part) making Peter's anguish palpable to the listener. That this text does not belong to the Gospel of John but was borrowed from Matthew suggests that Bach may have had a keen interest in it.

12c. (18.) Recitative (Evangelist, Peter, and Servant)

Er leugnete aber und sprach: Ich bins nicht. Spricht des Hohenpriesters Knecht' einer, ein Gefreundter des, dem Petrus das Ohr abgehauen hatte: Sahe ich dich nicht im Garten bei ihm? Da verleugnete Petrus abermal, und alsobald krähete der Hahn. Da gedachte Petrus an die Worte Jesu, und ging hinaus und weinete bitterlich.

But he denied it and said, "I am not." Then one of the high priest's servants, a relative of the one whose ear Peter had cut off, said, "Did I not see you in the garden with him?" Then Peter denied it again, and immediately the cock crowed. Then Peter remembered Jesus' words, and went outside, and wept bitterly.

In a technically demanding aria for tenor and string orchestra, the shattered narrator gives reign to absolute desperation, for Peter's act is now appropriated as his own. The music is full of dramatic leaps, jabbing rhythms, and sighing figures.

13. (19.) Tenor Aria

Ach, mein Sinn,	O my spirit,
wo willt du endlich hin,	where will you finally go?
wo soll ich mich erquikken?	Where do I find comfort?
Bleib ich hier,	Do I stay here?
oder wünsch ich mir	Or call on
Berg und Hügel auf den Rükken?	mountain and hill to bury me?
Bei der Welt ist gar kein Rat,	This world offers no counsel,
und im Herzen	and in my heart
stehn die Schmerzen	I face the agony
meiner Missetat,	of my transgression,
weil der Knecht	for the servant
den Herrn verleugnet hat.	has denied his lord.

In the chorale that concludes Part I the chorus once again joins the action directly, commenting on Peter's failure to remember Christ's warning that he would deny him three times. The words "one earnest look" allude to the denial account in the Gospel of Luke, which alone of the four Gospels reports that after the cock crowed, "the Lord turned and looked at Peter."

14. (20.) Chorale

Petrus, der nicht denkt zurück,	Peter, not thinking back,
seinen Gott verneinet,	denies his God,
der doch auf ein' ernsten Blick	but upon one earnest look,
bitterlichen weinet.	weeps bitterly.
Jesu, blikke mich auch an,	Jesus, look also at me
wenn ich nicht will büßen;	when I am slow to repent;
wenn ich Böses hab getan,	when I have done some evil
rühre mein Gewissen!	stir my conscience!

Part II

Part II, which came after the sermon in Bach's day, takes us through the remaining horrible events: the interrogation, flogging, and, finally, crucifixion of Jesus. The most important formal feature of Part II (already mentioned earlier) is the symmetrical shape of a central complex of choruses, recitatives, and arias, in which a central hymn-like movement is framed by paired outer movements. Symmetrical design is evident on more than one level, as the following diagram demonstrates.

Chorus (18b [29]): Nicht diesen, sondern Barrabam!
    Recitative (18c [30]): Barrabas aber war ein Mörder
        Bass Arioso (19 [31]): Betrachte, meine Seel
            Aria (20 [32]): Erwäge
        Recitative (21a [33]): Und die Kreigsknechte
Chorus (21b [34]) Sei gegrüßet

    Recitative (21c [35]): Und gaben ihn Backenstreiche
        Chorus (21d [36]): Kreuzige, kreuzige!
            Recitative (21e [37]): Pilatus sprach zu ihnen
        Chorus (21f [38]): Wir haben ein Gesetz
    Recitative (21g [39]): Da Pilatus das Wort hörete

            "Chorale" (22 [40]): Durch dein Gefängnis

    Recitative (23a [41]): Die Jüden aber schrieen
        Chorus (23b [42]): Lässest du diesen los
            Recitative (23c [43]): Da Pilatus das Wort hörete
        Chorus (23d [44]): Weg, weg mit dem
    Recitative (23e [45]): Spricht Pilatus zu ihnen

Chorus (23f [46]): Wir haben keinen König
    Recitative (23g [47]): Da überantwortete er ihn
        Bass Aria and Chorus (24 [48]) Eilt, ihr angefochten Seelen
    Recitative (25a [49]): Allda kreuzigten sie ihn
Chorus (25b [50]) Schreibe nicht

Robin Leaver calls the central "chorale" movement the "heart and focus of the entire work." It might more accurately be called a "quasi-chorale" because the text is not a chorale text. Nevertheless, by setting the words to a well-known chorale melody, Bach gives the movement the liturgical weight of a chorale—a corporate expression of the congregation.

Why is this text so important that Bach would frame it with the "crucify" statements of the mob, as if imprisoned by the cries? Apparently, for Bach, the words captured "the essential meaning [of] the Passion story . . . that Jesus' submission to earthly bondage released humanity from eternal bondage."[14]

Bach often used arch form (palindromic symmetry) to structure his works. Examples include the motet "Jesu, meine Freude," Cantatas 75 and 76 (the first two cantatas Bach presented after arriving in Leipzig), and the *Mass in B Minor*, among others. In such works Bach evidently used arch form to draw attention to a central "keystone" movement, which often also functions as a turning point—a fulcrum. In literary and theological terms the central movement reveals the heart or "crux" of the matter. Arch form is therefore essentially chiastic, the movements forming the Greek letter *chi* (X):

$$
\begin{array}{ccc}
A & B & C \\
  & D &   \\
C & B & A
\end{array}
$$

When comparing instances of chiastic form in Bach's works we find that the central movements often mark a place where antithetical text elements meet; a turning point where paradoxical elements are resolved through a process of inversion. In theological terms it is the "cross principle": as Christ gained victory through his death so Christian believers are exalted through cross-bearing. Listeners in Bach's day would have known that the formulation of the concept originated with Jesus, who taught his disciples, "Unless a grain of wheat fall into the ground and die, it remains alone, but if it die it produces much fruit"[15] and "If any man would come after me, let him deny himself and take up his cross and follow me. For whoever would save his life will lose it, and whoever loses his life for my sake will find it."[16]

Part II of the *St. John Passion* begins with a chorale that hints at the paradox of the cross. Its primary focus, however, is the rank injustice of the preceding events. The simple hymn serves as a banner for the entire second part.

15. (21.) Chorale

Christus, der uns selig macht,	Christ, through whom we are blest,
kein Bös' hat begangen,	knew no evildoing.
der ward für uns in der Nacht	He for us was in the night
als ein Dieb gefangen,	like a thief arrested,
geführt vor gottlose Leut	led before a godless throng
und fälschlich verklaget,	and falsely accused,
verlacht, verhöhnt und verspeit,	laughed at, scoffed at, spat on,
wie denn die Schrift saget.	as it says in the scriptures.

Now the case is transferred to Roman authority and Pilate comes on stage.

16a. (22.) Recitative (Evangelist and Pilate)

Da führeten sie Jesum von Kaiphas vor das Richthaus, und es war frühe. Und sie gingen nicht in das Richthaus, auf daß sie nicht unrein würden, sondern Ostern essen möchten. Da ging Pilatus zu ihnen heraus und sprach: Was bringet ihr für Klage wider diesen Menschen? Sie antworteten und sprachen zu ihm:

Then they led Jesus from Caiaphas into the courthouse, and it was early. And they did not enter the courthouse, lest they become defiled, for they wanted to eat the Passover. Then Pilate went out to them, and said, "What charges do you bring against this person?" They answered and said to him:

The mob hardly waits for Pilate to finish speaking and its response begs the question. The crowd's increasing determination can be heard in the chromatically ascending "stalking" motive of the voices, and the threat of crucifixion in the ♫ "crucify" motive, which appears in the latter part of the movement.

16b. (23.) Chorus

Wäre dieser nicht ein Übeltäter, wir hätten dir ihn nicht überantwortet.

If this man were not an evildoer, we would not have brought him before you.

Pilate tries to extricate himself by deferring to religious law, but the mob responds, "We may not put someone to death." In this way we learn for the first time that Jesus is being accused of a capital crime.

16c. (24.) Recitative (Evangelist and Pilate)

Da sprach Pilatus zu ihnen: So nehmet ihr hin und richtet ihn nach eurem Gesetze! Da sprachen die Jüden zu ihm:

Then Pilate said to them, "So take him and judge him according to your law!" Then the Jews said to him:

Again Bach connects narrative recitative and choral outburst, underlining the intensity of the exchange. The "stalking" motive returns, while the flutes and first violins play continuous, leaping sixteenths, denoting the increased agitation of the accusers.

16d. (25.) Chorus

Wir dürfen niemand töten.

We are not allowed to put anyone to death.

At this point the St. John Gospel account stresses again the preordained nature of these events. Pilate questions Jesus regarding his kingship and Jesus answers majestically, "My kingdom is not of this world." When he continues, "If my kingdom were of this world my servants would fight . . ." the agitated style of the previous movement reappears briefly in both vocal and accompanying parts, effectively highlighting the contrast between human and divine perspectives. Since Jesus claims an other-worldly kingdom, Pilate now has no excuse.

16e. (26.) Recitative (Evangelist, Pilate, and Jesus)

Auf daß erfüllet würde das Wort Jesu, welches er sagte, da er deutete, welches Todes er sterben würde. Da ging Pilatus wieder hinein in das Richthaus und rief Jesu und sprach zu ihm: Bist du der Jüden König? Jesus antwortete: Redest du das von dir selbst, oder habens dir andere von mir gesagt? Pilatus antwortete: Bin ich ein Jüde? Dein Volk und die Hohenpriester haben dich mir überantwortet; was hast du getan? Jesus antwortete: Mein Reich ist nicht von dieser Welt; wäre mein Reich von dieser Welt, meine Diener würden darob kämpfen, daß ich den Jüden nicht überantwortet würde; aber, nun ist mein Reich nicht von dannen.	So that the word of Jesus might be fulfilled, which he had spoken, when he had indicated by what manner of death he would die. Then Pilate entered the courthouse again and called Jesus, and said to him, "Are you the king of the Jews?" Jesus answered, "Are you saying this of yourself, or have others said this to you of me?" Pilate answered, "Am I a Jew? Your people and the high priests have given you over to me; what have you done?" Jesus answered, "My kingdom is not of this world; if my kingdom were of this world my servants would fight to defend it, so that I would not be delivered over to the Jews! But now my kingdom is not from thence.

The choir takes up the theme of Christ's kingship in two stanzas of a hymn. Beginning as it does with the divine appellation, "Ach großer König," this movement parallels the earlier chorale, "O große Lieb." To stress the connection between the two, Bach uses the same chorale tune for both texts.

17. (27.) Chorale

Ach großer König, groß zu allen Zeiten, wie kann ich gnugsam diese Treu ausbreiten? Keins Menschen Herze mag indes ausdenken, was dir zu schenken.	O mighty king, mighty through all ages, how can I fitly proclaim this faithfulness? No human heart can ever conceive what to give you.
Ich kann's mit meinen Sinnen nicht erreichen, womit doch dein Erbarmen zu vergleichen. Wie kann ich dir denn deine Liebestaten im Werk erstatten?	With all my faculties I can not conceive what might compare with your compassion. How then could I, repay your deeds of love, with works?

As Pilate continues to press him for answers, Jesus turns the conversation to the issue most fundamental to the question of his identity and the trial at hand: integrity and the honest search for truth. Pilate, realizing that he has an innocent man on his hands, seeks to release him. However, his offer of amnesty for the so-called King of the Jews simply enrages the crowd and they shout that they would rather have the release of a notorious criminal named Barabbas.

18a. (28.) Recitative (Evangelist, Pilate, and Jesus)

Da sprach Pilatus zu ihm: So bist du dennoch ein König? Jesus antwortete: Du sagsts, ich bin ein König. Ich bin dazu geboren und in die Welt kommen, daß ich die Wahrheit zeugen soll. Wer aus der Wahrheit ist, der höret meine Stimme. Spricht Pilatus zu ihm: Was ist Wahrheit?

Then Pilate said to him, "So you are nevertheless a king?" Jesus answered, "You say, I am a king. For that I was born and have come into the world, that I should bear witness to the truth. Whoever is of the truth hears my voice. Pilate said to him, "What is truth?"

Und da er das gesaget, ging er wieder hinaus, zu den Jüden und spricht zu ihnen: Ich find keine Schuld an ihm. Ihr habt aber eine Gewohnheit, daß ich euch einen losgebe: wollt ihr nun, daß ich euch der Jüden König losgebe? Da schrieen sie wieder allesamt und sprachen:

And when he said this he went out again to the Jews and said to them, "I find no fault in him. But you have a custom, that I release one person to you: do you wish for me to release to you the king of the Jews?" But again they all shouted and said:

Bach's setting of the crowd's retort is short and effective with its jabbing vocal lines and hectic obbligato played by Flutes I and II, Oboe I, and Violin I.

18b. (29.) Chorus

Nicht diesen, sondern Barrabam! Not this one but Barabbas!

From the chorus Bach plunges directly into a recitative. That he wanted the dramatic momentum maintained at this point is clear from the final notes of the obbligato and bass instruments, which are sustained, providing a bridge between the two movements. In the recitative the narrator first explains the egregiousness of the crowd's choice; then, with a technically demanding flurry of notes, he paints a vivid picture of the flogging ordered by Pilate.

18c. (30.) Recitative (Evangelist)

Barrabas aber war ein Mörder. Da nahm Pilatus Jesum und geißelte ihn. Barabbas, however, was a murderer. Then Pilate took Jesus and scourged him.

From a dramatic perspective, the following bass arioso marks the first moment of acquiescence. It is distinctive for its accompaniment: the motoric rhythms of a plucked lute and intermittently sounding bass—like the ticking of a clock—suggest resignation, a mood accentuated by softly sighing strings (played by muted violins or viola d'amores). Concerning this instrumentation Marion Metcalf notes that the lute was considered antiquated in Bach's time, and that "this particular combination of instruments and voice is unique in what survives of Bach's music."[17] Nevertheless, lutes were apparently used as continuo instruments in Leipzig's church music and are specified in at least one other cantata.[18]

19. (31.) Bass Arioso

Betrachte, meine Seel,	Consider, my soul,
mit ängstlichem Vergnügen,	with fearful pleasure,
mit bittrer Lust	with bitter delight
und halb beklemmtem Herzen	and half constricted heart,
dein höchstes Gut	your greatest good
in Jesu Schmerzen,	in Jesus' suffering;
wie dir auf Dornen,	how for you the thorns
so ihn stechen,	that pierce him,
die Himmelsschlüsselblumen blühn!	bloom with heaven's primroses!
Du kannst viel süße Frucht	You can gather much sweet fruit
von seiner Wermut brechen,	amongst his wormwood,
drum sieh ohn Unterlaß auf ihn!	so look unceasingly upon him!

In a coloratura da capo aria for tenor, the listener is reminded that these horrible events will end in blessing. The point is made in typically graphic baroque manner: the streaked blood stains on Jesus' back are compared to the rainbow of promise after the flood in Noah's day. The aria is much longer than the other ones in the *St. John Passion*, suggesting that Bach considered it of primary significance.

20. (32.) Tenor Aria

Erwäge,	Ponder,
wie sein blutgefärbter Rükken	how his bloodied back,
in allen Stükken	in every way
dem Himmel gleiche geht,	is like the heavens,
daran, nachdem die Wasserwogen	on which after the watery billows
von unsrer Sündflut	of our sin's flood
sich verzogen,	have subsided,
der allerschönste Regenbogen	the most beautiful rainbow
als Gottes Gnadenzeichen steht.	appears, as a token of God's grace.

Having tortured him, the Roman soldiers begin to taunt Jesus, prancing around him in a mockingly playful dance for voices and instruments. The dance ends abruptly with further violence as they hit him in the face.

21a. (33.) Recitative (Evangelist)

Und die Kriegsknechte flochten eine Krone von Dornen und satzten sie auf sein Haupt und legten ihm ein Purpurkleid an und sprachen:	And the soldiers plaited a crown out of thorns, and set it on his head, and put a robe of purple on him, and said:

21b. (34.) Chorus

Sei gegrüßet, lieber Jüdenkönig!	We hail you, beloved King of the Jews!

Attempting to appeal to the humanity of the crowd, Pilate presents the innocent victim, now costumed in crown and robe, to the crowd. But the mob is bloodthirsty, and will have none of it.

21c. (35.) Recitative (Evangelist and Pilate)

Und gaben ihm Bakkenstreiche. Da ging Pilatus wieder heraus und sprach zu ihnen: Sehet, ich führe ihn heraus zu euch, daß ihr erkennet, daß ich keine Schuld an ihm finde.	And they hit him in the face. Then Pilate went out again and said to them, "Look, I bring him out to you, so that you know that I find no fault in him."
Also ging Jesus heraus und trug eine Dornenkrone und Purpurkleid. Und er sprach zu ihnen: Sehet, welch ein Mensch! Da ihn die Hohenpriester und die Diener sahen, schrieen sie und sprachen:	So Jesus went out wearing a crown of thorns and a robe of purple. And Pilate said to them, "Behold, the man!" When the high priests and servants saw him, they screamed and said:

Bach's musical portrayal of the enraged mob's response incorporates subtle complexities. Beyond a surface effect of sheer agitation, he encapsulates the idea of crucifixion by means of chiastic devices: invertible counterpoint (in which the ♫ "kreuzige" motive and a linear figure consisting of two sinuously clashing parallel lines exchange places) and motivic inversion (in which the primary motive appears in mirror form).

21d. (36.) Chorus

Kreuzige, kreuzige!	Crucify, crucify!

In an apparent bluff, Pilate tells the accusers they will have to carry out the deed themselves.

21e. (37.) Recitative (Evangelist and Pilate)

Pilatus sprach zu ihnen: Nehmet ihr ihn hin und kreuziget ihn; denn ich finde keine Schuld an ihm! Die Jüden antworteten ihm:	Pilate said to them, "You take him away and crucify him, for I find no fault in him." The Jews answered him:

For their reply Bach employs an emphatic rhythm with syncopation to provide "a rather pompous air to the assertion that Jesus has broken Jewish law; with minor rhythmic variations, the same theme in No. 23b (42) suggests a more frantic response to the possibility of Jesus' release."[19] The form is that of fugue, in which voices follow each other in strict imitation. Because fugue form was often used to depict law or dogma, its appearance here is ironic, for the mob is anything but lawful in its inflexible fanaticism. Nevertheless, the crowd does get to the heart of the complaint: Jesus' claim to divinity.

21f. (38.) Chorus

Wir haben ein Gesetz, und nach dem   We have a law, and according to that law
Gesetz soll er sterben; denn er hat sich   he must die, for he has made himself out
selbst zu Gottes Sohn gemacht.   to be God's son.

Pilate is now afraid, and when Jesus refuses to cower despite Pilate's threats he is frightened even more. Pilate's eventual determination to find a way to release his prisoner is portrayed by Bach in harmonies of utmost sweetness, as if to suggest that a happy outcome might yet be possible. However the music page is littered with sharp signs (in German the sharp sign is called "Kreuz," which is also the word for "cross") as if to say that it will never happen.

21g. (39.) Recitative (Evangelist, Pilate, and Jesus)

Da Pilatus das Wort hörete, fürchtet' er   Now when Pilate heard this he was even
sich noch mehr und ging wieder hinein in   more frightened, and entered the court-
das Richthaus, und sprach zu Jesu: Von   house again, and said to Jesus, "From
wannen bist du? Aber Jesus gab ihm   where are you?" But Jesus gave him no
keine Antwort. Da sprach Pilatus zu ihm: answer. Then Pilate said to him, "Do you
Redest du nicht mit mir? Weißest du   refuse to speak to me?" Do not know
nicht, daß ich Macht habe, dich zu   that I have the power to crucify you, and
kreuzigen, und Macht habe, dich loszu-   the power to release you?" Jesus re-
geben? Jesus antwortete: Du hättest   plied, "You would have no power over
keine Macht über mich, wenn sie dir   me if it were not given to you from
nicht wäre von oben herab gegeben;   above; therefore, he who delivered me
darum, der mich dir überantwortet hat,   up to you has the greater sin." From then
der hat's größ're Sünde. Von dem an   on Pilate strove for a way to release him.
trachtete Pilatus, wie er ihn losließe.

We come now to the central movement, which is, literally and figuratively, the crux of the matter—the theology of the cross in a nutshell. The hymn text relates directly to the theme expressed at the very outset of the work: "Show us by your Passion that you, the true Son of God, were glorified at all times, even in the greatest abasement." From a dramatic point of view, too, this chorale is the pivotal point in the work. Until now there has still been hope that Jesus might be released. The mob, however, is uncontrollable in its murderous intent, and the turning point is reached.

22. (40.) Chorale

Durch dein Gefängnis, Gottes Sohn,
muß uns die Freiheit kommen;
Dein Kerker ist der Gnadenthron,
die Freistatt aller Frommen;
denn gingst du nicht
die Knechtschaft ein,
müßt unsre Knechtschaft ewig sein.

Through your captivity O Son of God,
our freedom had to come;
your prison is the throne of grace,
the free state of all the godly;
for had you not
taken up servitude,
our servitude would have been eternal.

The rabble now aggressively pushes its advantage, threatening Pilate with sibilant language that veritably hisses in anger.

23a. (41.) Recitative (Evangelist)

Die Jüden aber schrieen und sprachen:

But the Jews screamed and said:

23b. (42.) Chorus

Lässest du diesen los, so bist du des Kaisers Freund nicht; denn wer sich zum Könige machet, der ist wider den Kaiser.

If you let this man go, you are no friend of Caesar, for whoever makes himself out to be a king is against Caesar.

Pilate is not cowed by the crowd. In a show of judicial authority he ironically presents Jesus as their king. In so doing he turns the accusers' own argument against them, making them liable for treason themselves.

23c. (43.) Recitative (Evangelist and Pilate)

Da Pilatus das Wort hörete, führete er Jesum heraus und satzte sich auf den Richtstuhl, an der Stätte, die da heißet: Hochpflaster, auf Ebräisch aber: Gabbatha. Es war aber der Rüsttag in Ostern, um die sechste Stunde, und er spricht zu den Jüden: Sehet, das ist euer König! Sie schrieen aber:

When Pilate heard these words, he led Jesus out, and sat down on the seat of judgment, in a place called High Pavement, but in Hebrew called Gabbatha. It was about the sixth hour on the day of preparation for the Passover, and he said to the Jews, "Look, that is your king!" But they shouted:

In response, the frenzied crowd calls for crucifixion a second time. The "crucify" motive reappears, reminding us of the earlier statement. At the end of the agitated movement the discord reaches a climax with the choral basses holding a high C♯ against clashing B♯s and D♯s in the other parts.

23d. (44.) Chorus

Weg mit dem, kreuzige ihn!

Away with him, crucify him!

23e. (45.) Recitative (Evangelist and
Pilate)

Spricht Pilatus zu ihnen: Soll ich euren König kreuzigen? Die Hohenpriester antworteten:	Pilate said to them, "Shall I crucify your king?" The high priests answered:

After Pilate taunts them with a further reference to "Jesus their king" they shout their avowed allegiance to Caesar.

23f. (46.) Chorus

Wir haben keinen König denn den Kaiser.	We have no king but Caesar.

In a highly chromatic recitative (all twelve tones of the octave appear in the vocal part within six measures) the narrator describes Jesus' sentencing. Crucifixion was a particularly brutal form of execution and Bach sets the entire text very expressively; in particular, he gives the word "crucify" a striking melisma of great pathos.

23g. (47.) Recitative (Evangelist)

Da überantwortete er ihn, daß er gekreuziget würde. Sie nahmen aber Jesum and führeten ihn hin. Und er trug sein Kreuz und ging hinaus zur Stätte, die da heißet Schädelstätt, welche heißet auf Ebräisch: Golgatha.	Then Pilate handed him over so that he might be crucified. But they took Jesus and led him away. And, carrying his cross, he went out to a place called Place of a Skull, which, in Hebrew, is called Golgotha.

Evidently the crowd immediately begins to disperse, eager to tell others of the verdict and the impending execution. Bach paints the picture vividly with unison figures that run up the scale. The exhortation to run to Golgotha is both literal and figurative. In the figurative sense, the soloist urges listeners, as human beings driven and assailed by cares, to run to the cross in faith. The text stresses what has been emphasized from the midpoint of the Passion on: the cross ultimately represents the means of salvation. Marion Metcalf writes, "In [this aria] Bach again reinforces the Easter message, as the bass soloist urges seekers of salvation, represented by the chorus asking 'where? where?,' to look [to] Golgotha, where Jesus was crucified."[20]

24. (48.) Bass Aria and **Chorus**

Eilt, ihr angefochtnen Seelen, geht aus euren Marterhöhlen, eilt,	Hasten, you souls assailed, leave your caves of torment, hasten,
Wohin?	Where to?
eilt nach Golgatha! Nehmet an des Glaubens Flügel, flieht,	hasten to Golgotha! Take on the wings of faith, fly,

Wohin?	Where to?
flieht zum Kreuzeshügel,	fly to the cross's hill,
eure Wohlfahrt blüht allda!	your welfare blossoms there!

The actual crucifixion is told simply—without graphic description. More pointed is the writer's description of Pilate's parting jab at his unruly subjects: on Jesus' cross he hangs a taunting sign (in three languages) that combines a reference to Jesus' lowly origin with the facetiously bestowed royal title. To highlight the inscription's significance, Bach sets it majestically with a plagal ("Amen") cadence in A♭ major.

25a. (49.) Recitative (Evangelist)

Allda kreuzigten sie ihn, und mit ihm zween andere zu beiden Seiten, Jesum aber mitten inne. Pilatus aber schrieb eine Überschrift, und satzte sie auf das Kreuz, und war geschrieben: "Jesus von Nazareth, der Jüden König." Diese Überschrift lasen viel Jüden, denn die Stätte war nahe bei der Stadt, da Jesus gekreuziget ist. Und es war geschrieben auf ebräische, griechische und lateinische Sprache. Da sprachen die Hohenpriester der Jüden zu Pilato:

There they crucified him, and with him two others on either side, Jesus between them. But Pilate wrote an inscription and put it on the cross. It said: "Jesus of Nazareth, King of the Jews!" This inscription was read by many Jews, for the place where Jesus was crucified was near to the town. And it was written in Hebrew, Greek, and Latin. Then the high priests of the Jews said to Pilate:

Of course the religious leaders object strenuously and suggest an alternative reading.

25b. (50.) Chorus

Schreibe nicht: der Jüden König, sondern daß er gesaget habe: Ich bin der Jüden König!

Do not write "The King of the Jews" but rather that he said, 'I am the King of the Jews!'"

Again Pilate asserts his authority.

25c. (51.) Recitative (Evangelist and Pilate)

Pilatus antwortet: Was ich geschrieben habe, das habe ich geschrieben.

Pilate replied, "What I have written, that I have written."

Providing some respite from the intensity of the foregoing exchange, the chorus sings a simple hymn that ponders the significance of Jesus' name and cross for the believer.

26. (52.) Chorale
In meines Herzens Grunde,
dein Nam und Kreuz allein
funkelt all Zeit und Stunde,
drauf kann ich fröhlich sein.
Erschein mir in dem Bilde
zu Trost in meiner Not,
wie du, Herr Christ, so milde
dich hast geblut' zu Tod!

In my heart's center
your name and cross alone
glows at all times and hours;
for this I can be joyful.
Appear to me in that image
(for comfort in my need)
of how you, Lord Christ, so gently
bled to death for us!

The four soldiers, considering Jesus as good as dead, divide his clothes among themselves.

27a. (53.) Recitative (Evangelist)
Die Kriegsknechte aber, da sie Jesum gekreuziget hatten, nahmen seine Kleider und machten vier Teile, einem jeglichen Kriegsknechte sein Teil, dazu auch den Rock. Der Rock aber war ungenähet, von oben an gewürket durch und durch. Da sprachen sie untereinander:

But the soldiers, when they had crucified Jesus, divided his garments in four equal portions, a portion for each of the soldiers, and also his coat. Now the coat had no seams but was woven through and through from end to end. So they said to one another:

Realizing that the coat is too precious to be cut, the soldiers decide to gamble for it. Bach's music rollicks along, the instruments perhaps depicting the rattling roll of dice. The competition becomes more intense. Finally, yelping with success, the soprano (the youngest one?) grabs the prize with glee.

27b. (54.) Chorus
Lasset uns den nicht zerteilen, sondern darum losen, wes er sein soll.

Let us not divide it, but draw lots for it to see whose it shall be.

In keeping with the Gospel writer's aim to depict these horrible events as divinely supervised, he notes that the soldiers' act was, in fact, a fulfillment of prophecy, and he quotes a passage from Psalm 22 to prove it. He then describes the attending women (which include three named Mary) and the disciples, who stand at the foot of the cross. Then he relates one of the most moving exchanges in the entire Passion account: in a weak voice Jesus asks the "disciple whom Jesus loved" (i.e., John, the Gospel writer himself) and his mother to care for each other when he is gone.

27c. (55.) Recitative (Evangelist and Jesus)

Auf daß erfüllet würde die Schrift, die da saget: "Sie haben meine Kleider unter sich geteilet und haben über meinen Rock das Los geworfen." Solches taten die Kriegesknechte.

So that the scripture might be fulfilled, which says, "They parted my raiment among them and cast lots for my coat." That is what the soldiers did.

Es stund aber bei dem Kreuze Jesu seine Mutter und seiner Mutter Schwester, Maria, Kleophas Weib, und Maria Magdalena. Da nun Jesus seine Mutter sahe und den Jünger dabei stehen, den er lieb hatte, spricht er zu seiner Mutter: Weib, siehe, das ist dein Sohn! Darnach spricht er zu dem Jünger: Siehe, das ist deine Mutter!

Now standing beside the cross of Jesus were his mother and his mother's sister, Mary the wife of Clopas, and Mary Magdalene. Now when Jesus saw his mother and his beloved disciple standing by her, he said to his mother, "Woman, behold, this is your son! Then he said to the disciple, "Behold, that is your mother!"

Emotionally spent, the chorus responds with a hymn of bittersweet simplicity. Bach uses the same tune here as in the earlier chorale, "Petrus, der nicht denkt zurrück." In this way he draws a comparison between Jesus' thoughtfulness—even in death—with Peter's thoughtlessness.

28. (56.) Chorale

Er nahm alles wohl in acht
in der letzten Stunde,
seine Mutter noch bedacht,
setzt ihr ein' Vormunde.
O Mensch, mache Richtigkeit,
Gott und Menschen liebe,
stirb darauf ohn alles Leid,
und dich nicht betrübe!

He took heed of everything
in his last hour,
thought yet of his mother,
assigning to her a guardian.
O man, act rightly,
love God and fellow man,
then die without sorrow,
and do not be distressed!

As Jesus nears his end the Gospel writer once again notes the prophetic nature of the transpiring events.

29. (57.) Recitative (Evangelist and Jesus)

Und von Stund an nahm sie der Jünger zu sich. Darnach, als Jesus wußte, daß schon alles vollbracht war, daß die Schrift erfüllet würde, spricht er: Mich dürstet! Da stund ein Gefäße voll Essigs. Sie fülleten aber einen Schwamm mit Essig und legten ihn um einen Isopen, und hielten es ihm dar zum Munde. Da nun Jesus den Essig genommen hatte, sprach er: Es ist vollbracht!

And from that hour on the disciple took her to himself. After that, when Jesus knew that everything had already been finished to fulfill scripture, he said, "I thirst!" A vessel full of vinegar stood there. They filled a sponge with vinegar and put it on a twig of hyssop, and held it to his mouth. When Jesus had taken the vinegar he said, "It is finished!"

The double meaning of the phrase, "It is finished" is taken up in a highly memorable aria that follows. Of this movement, Martin Geck writes:

> Bach's utter centrality in the history of Western music is nowhere better illustrated than by the aria "Es ist vollbracht," the principal idea of which is derived from the tradition of the instrumental *tombeau* as scored for lute, harpsichord and viol and associated at least from the seventeenth century with the notion of commemorating the death of important individuals. . . . At the same time, however, the opening bars of the aria anticipate the *Klagender Gesang* ("Arioso dolente") of Beethoven's op. 110 Piano Sonata and the aria "Es ist genug" ("It is enough") from Mendelssohn's Elijah.[21]

Andreas Glöckner writes:

> [Bach] again breaks the rules of the traditional da capo aria. Instead of using the usual A-B-A form, in which the middle section produces a clear contrast by virtue of its reduced volume of sound, Bach applies the opposite strategy in this unusual movement. While the tone of the A section is intentionally subdued through the use of the chamber musical forces of viola da gamba and continuo, Bach accentuates a sharp contrast in the B section—fitting the text "Der Held aus Juda siegt mit Macht"—by calling for the entire string section of the orchestra, which he then augmented in 1749 by the addition of a bassono grosso (contra-bassoon). The contrast is emphasized the more by the different tempo headings—"Molto Adagio" for the A section and "Vivace" for the B section.[22]

The idea that Christ's death accomplished a preordained plan of salvation is made explicit in the movement, as the alto meditates on Christ's final words, "It is finished." Michael Marissen writes:

> Bach's aria "Es ist vollbracht" (No. 30 [58]) projects Luther's theology of the cross most forcefully. At first it seems as though the notes simply contradict the words, since Jesus' cry of triumph is set as a somber dirge. But these are surface features. The aria is scored with an obbligato for a special instrument, the viola da gamba, a favorite solo instrument in French Baroque court music; and often the underlying rhythms are the ones cultivated in the majestic style of Louis XIV's court music and therefore widely imitated elsewhere. . . . Although it is notated in [this so-called] dotted style, [the] gamba music, owing to its slowness and smoothness, sounds somber. That is to say, only on the page, which listeners do not see, does the music appear majestic. As

Bach's music has it, then, Jesus' majesty is "hidden" in its opposite, which is very much a Lutheran approach.

[By contrast] the middle section of this aria . . . [with its] fast repeated notes, an Italian Baroque convention for "militant" affects [i.e., emotional states] . . . is more what one would expect from a victorious Christ. But the final notes spell a diminished chord, the most unstable harmony available in Bach's vocabulary. This middle section cannot stand formally closed. . . . It has to resolve somehow, and it does so right into the slow gamba music of the opening section again.[23]

30. (58.) Alto Aria

Es ist vollbracht!	It is finished!
O Trost für die gekränkten Seelen.	O comfort for all vexed souls.
Die Trauernacht,	The night of grieving
läßt nun die letzte Stunde zählen.	now sees its final hour.
Der Held aus Juda	The champion from Judah
siegt mit Macht,	triumphs mightily
und schließt den Kampf.	and ends the battle.
Es ist vollbracht.	It is finished.

The actual death of Jesus is set very simply—the tenor soloist is given the challenge of conveying the utmost pathos in just nine notes.

31. (59.) Recitative (Evangelist)

Und neiget das Haupt und verschied.	And bowed his head and was gone.

In a fascinating movement that combines a four-part chorale with a bass aria in the slowly rocking rhythm of the siciliano (a baroque dance with pastoral associations), we hear the inner struggle of the individual played out against the ecclesiastical response of the believing community.

32. (60.) Bass Aria and **Chorus**

Mein teurer Heiland, laß dich fragen,	My dear Savior, give me answer,
Jesu, der du warest tot,	Jesus, you who once were dead,
da du nunmehr ans Kreuz geschlagen	since you were nailed upon the cross,
und selbst gesaget: es ist vollbracht,	and said yourself, "It is finished,"
lebest nun ohn Ende,	now you live forever.
bin ich vom Sterben frei gemacht?	am I now freed from death?
in der letzten Todesnot	In the final pangs of death
nirgend mich hinwende	may I never turn elsewhere
Kann ich durch deine Pein und Sterben	Can I, through your pain and dying,
das Himmelreich ererben?	inherit the heavenly kingdom?
Ist aller Welt Erlösung da?	Is this the redemption of all the world?
als zu dir,	than to you,
der mich versühnt,	who have atoned for me,
o du lieber Herre!	O beloved Savior!

Du kannst vor Schmerzen	Indeed you cannot answer
zwar nichts sagen;	for pain;
Gib mir nur,	Grant me but
was du verdient,	what you have earned,
doch neigest du das Haupt	yet you bow your head
mehr ich nicht begehre!	more I do not desire!
und sprichst stillschweigend: ja.	to say, in silence, "Yes."

Borrowed from the Gospel of Matthew, the earthquake scene that follows was apparently incorporated into the libretto at Bach's own wish. In both recitative and aria the composer paints a vivid picture in the instrumental lines of the quake and the rending of the temple veil, with shaking figures and a two-octave run that tears downward in thirty-second notes.

33. (61.) Recitative (Evangelist)

Und siehe da, der Vorhang im Tempel	And behold, the veil in the temple was
zerriß in zwei Stück von oben an bis	torn in two pieces, from top to bottom.
unten aus. Und die Erde erbebete, und	And the earth shook, and the rocks were
die Felsen zerrissen, und die Gräber	torn apart, and graves were opened, and
täten sich auf, und stunden auf viele	the bodies of many saints arose.
Leiber der Heiligen.	

Musing that the cataclysmic events (which are now depicted even more explicitly in the instrumental lines) constitute nature's horrified response to the death of its creator, the tenor asks with great earnestness what the heart's response to Jesus' death should be.

34. (62.) Tenor Arioso

Mein Herz, indem die ganze Welt	O my heart, now that all the world
bei Jesu Leiden gleichfalls leidet,	at Jesus' suffering likewise suffers:
die Sonne sich in Trauer kleidet,	the sun shrouds itself in mourning,
der Vorhang reißt,	the veil tears,
der Fels zerfällt,	the rocks disintegrate,
die Erde bebt,	the earth shakes,
die Gräber spalten,	the graves split open,
weil sie den Schöpfer sehn erkalten,	because they see the Creator dying;
was willst du deines Ortes tun?	what will you for your part do?

It is the soprano who answers the tenor's question with an aria in F minor, a lament in which restless thirty-second notes, a throbbing bass figure (consisting of repeated eighth notes that begin after an initial eighth note rest on the downbeat of each measure), sighing gestures, and occasional pauses work together to produce a vivid portrayal of grief and anguish.

35. (63.) Soprano Aria

Zerfließe, mein Herze,	Overflow, O my heart,
in Fluten der Zähren,	in torrents of tears,
dem Höchsten zu Ehren!	to honor the Most High!
Erzähle der Welt und dem	Tell earth
Himmel die Not:	and heaven the dark tidings:
dein Jesus ist tot!	your Jesus is dead!

In a lengthy recitative by the Evangelist we encounter again the Gospel writer's concern to portray Jesus' crucifixion as a divine fulfillment of Old Testament scriptures, which are highlighted musically by Bach in passages marked "Adagio."

36. (64.) Recitative (Evangelist)

Die Jüden aber, dieweil es der Rüsttag war, daß nicht die Leichname am Kreuze blieben den Sabbat über (denn desselbigen Sabbaths Tag war sehr groß), baten sie Pilatum, daß ihre Beine gebrochen und sie abgenommen würden. Da kamen die Kriegsknechte und brachen dem ersten die Beine und dem andern, der mit ihm gekreuziget war. Als sie aber zu Jesu kamen, da sie sahen, daß er schon gestorben war, brachen sie ihm die Beine nicht; sondern der Kriegsknechte einer eröffnete seine Seite mit einem Speer, und alsobald ging Blut und Wasser heraus.

But the Jews, because it was the day of preparation, so that the body should not remain on the cross over the Sabbath (for that Sabbath was a very high one), entreated Pilate to have their legs broken and they be taken down. Then the soldiers came and broke the legs of the first one, and of the other who was crucified with him. But when they came to Jesus and saw that he had already died, they did not break his legs; instead, one of the soldiers opened his side with a spear, and immediately blood and water came out.

Und der das gesehen hat, der hat es bezeuget, und sein Zeugnis ist wahr, und derselbige weiß, daß er die Wahrheit saget, auf das ihr glaubet. Denn solches ist geschehen, auf daß die Schrift erfüllet würde: "Ihr sollet ihm kein Bein zerbrechen." Und abermal spricht eine andere Schrift: "Sie werden sehen, in welchen sie gestochen haben."

And the one who saw this has borne record, and he knows that he is speaking the truth, so that you may believe. For these things happened so that the scripture might be fulfilled, "You shall not break one of his legs." Again another scripture says, "They will behold the one whom they have pierced."

Here Bach reintroduces the chorale tune of *Christus der uns selig macht*, which began Part II of the Passion. In this way he comes full circle, inviting the listener to contemplate the parallel sentiments of the two hymns.

37. (65.) Chorale

O hilf, Christe, Gottes Sohn,	Help, O Christ, God's Son,
durch dein bitter Leiden,	through your bitter suffering,
daß wir dir stets untertan	that we, remaining subject to you always,
all Untugend meiden,	would avoid all wickedness;

deinen Tod und sein Ursach	would always contemplate beneficially
fruchtbarlich bedenken,	your death and its purpose; bring you
dafür, wiewohl arm und schwach,	offerings of thanksgiving for it,
dir Dankopfer schenken!	though they be poor and weak!

Having prayed for strength to overcome human weakness in the preceding chorale, the librettist now tells the account of Jesus' burial, in which two disciples—formerly too timid to come forward and be identified as such—play a central role.

38. (66.) Recitative (Evangelist)

Darnach bat Pilatum Joseph von Arimathia, der ein Jünger Jesu war (doch heimlich aus Furcht vor den Jüden), daß er möchte abnehmen den Leichnam Jesu. Und Pilatus erlaubete es. Derowegen kam er und nahm den Leichnam Jesu herab.

Afterward, Joseph of Arimathea, who was a disciple of Jesus (but secretly, fearing the Jews), asked Pilate if he might take down Jesus' body. And Pilate allowed it. So he came and took down Jesus' body.

Es kam aber auch Nikodemus, der vormals bei der Nacht zu Jesu kommen war, und brachte Myrrhen und Aloen unter einander bei hundert Pfunden. Da nahmen sie den Leichnam Jesu und bunden ihn in leinen Tücher mit Spezereien, wie die Jüden pflegen zu begraben. Es war aber an der Stätte, da er gekreuziget ward, ein Garte, und im Garten ein neu Grab, in welches niemand je geleget war. Daselbst hin legten sie Jesum, um des Rüsttags willen der Jüden, dieweil das Grab nahe war.

There came also Nicodemus, who had earlier come to Jesus by night, and brought a mixture of myrrh and aloes, a hundred pounds' weight. Then they took Jesus' body and wound it in linen cloths with spices, as is the Jewish manner of burial. Now at the place where he was crucified, there was a garden, and in the garden a new grave, in which no one had ever been laid. There they laid Jesus, since it was the day of preparation, the grave being close by.

Following convention, and in the interest of large-scale symmetry, Bach ends the work with a major chorus, a gentle lullaby that contemplates Jesus being laid to rest in the tomb. The length of the movement suggests that Bach found the text particularly meaningful, made all the more poignant, perhaps, by memories of the many children he had personally laid to rest. Apparently the librettist considered the movement inconclusive, however. To expand on the Christian believer's hope, which lies ultimately not in Christ's death but in the resurrection, a final chorale was added, allowing the believing community to affirm its anticipation of this eschatological event.

39. (67.) Chorus

Ruht wohl,	Rest, well,
ihr heiligen Gebeine,	you sacred bones,
die ich nun weiter nicht beweine,	over which I shall no further weep.
ruht wohl,	Rest well,
und bringt auch mich zur Ruh.	and bring me also to rest.
Das Grab, so euch bestimmet ist	The grave, destined for you,
und ferner keine Not umschließt,	and which no further pain encloses,
macht mir den Himmel auf	opens heaven for me,
und schließt die Hölle zu.	and closes hell.

40. (68.) Chorale

Ach Herr, laß dein lieb Engelein	O Lord, let your little angel dear,
am letzten End die Seele mein	in the final end, carry my soul
in Abrahams Schoß tragen,	into Abraham's bosom.
den Leib	Let this body rest
in seim Schlafkämmerlein	in its little sleeping chamber,
gar sanft ohn einge Qual und Pein	quite softly, without any torment or pain,
ruhn bis am jüngsten Tage!	until Judgment Day!
Alsdenn vom Tod erwekke mich,	And then from death awaken me,
daß meine Augen sehen dich	that my eyes may see you,
in aller Freud, o Gottes Sohn,	in full joy, O Son of God,
mein Heiland und Genadenthron!	my Savior and my mercyseat!
Herr Jesu Christ, erhöre mich,	Lord Jesus Christ, hear me,
ich will dich preisen ewiglich!	and I will praise you eternally!

Notes

1. Werner Braun, "Passion. 6. Eighteenth Century," in *New Grove Dictionary of Music and Musicians*, 2d ed., ed. Stanley Sadie (London: Macmillan, 2001), 19:208.

2. Martin Geck, trans. Stewart Spencer, CD booklet, J. S. Bach, *Johannes-Passion*, Concentus musicus Wien (Nikolaus Harnoncourt, conductor), Teldek 9031-74862-2, pp. 14–15.

3. Robin Leaver, "Passion," in *Oxford Composer Companions: J. S. Bach*, ed. Malcolm Boyd (Oxford: Oxford University Press, 1999), 361.

4. Marion Metcalf, "J. S. Bach: *Johannes Passion*," March 11, 2000, notes for the Alexandria Choral Society's 1985 performance of the *St. John Passion*, reprinted in remembrance of Marion R. Metcalf, formerly a member of the society, http://www.alexchoralsociety.org/bachnotes.htm (accessed June 23, 2004).

5. Andreas Glöckner, "Bach's *St. John Passion* and Its Different Versions," CD booklet, J. S. Bach, *St. John Passion*, Gächinger Kantorei, Bach-Collegium Stuttgart (Helmuth Rilling, conductor), Hänssler CD 92.075, pp. 68–69.

6. John Butt, "St. John Passion," in *Oxford Composer Companions: J. S. Bach*, ed. Malcolm Boyd (Oxford: Oxford University Press, 1999), 427.

7. Audrey Wong and Norm Proctor, "St. John Passion," July 7, 2003, http://www.bcg.org/Program_Notes/StJohn_694.html (accessed June 24, 2004).

8. Robin A. Leaver, "The Mature Vocal Works," *The Cambridge Companion to Bach*, ed. John Butt (Cambridge: Cambridge University Press, 1997), 100; John Butt, "St. John Passion" in Boyd, *Oxford Composer Companions: J. S. Bach*, 427–28.

9. Metcalf, "J. S. Bach: *Johannes Passion.*"

10. Wong and Proctor, "St. John Passion."

11. Published by Oxford University Press, 1998.

12. The first number follows the numbering system used in the new critical edition of Bach's works: *Johann Sebastian Bach: Neue Bach-Ausgabe sämtlicher Werke* (*NBA*), ed. Johann-Sebastian-Bach-Institut Göttingen, and Bach-Archiv Leipzig (Leipzig and Kassel, 1954–). The second number (in parentheses) follows the system used in the *Bach-Werke-Verzeichnis* (BWV); see Wolfgang Schmieder, *Thematisches Verzeichnis der musikalischen Werke von Johann Sebastian Bach*, rev. & expanded ed. (Wiesbaden: Breitkopf and Härtel, 1990).

13. Geck, *Johannes-Passion*, 15.

14. Metcalf, "J. S. Bach: *Johannes Passion.*"

15. John 12:24, Revised Standard Version.

16. Matthew 16:24–25, Revised Standard Version.

17. Metcalf, "J. S. Bach: *Johannes Passion.*"

18. Karl Hochreither, trans. Melvin P. Unger, *Performance Practice of the Instrumental-Vocal Works of Johann Sebastian Bach* (Lanham, Md.: Scarecrow Press, 2002), 7.

19. Melcalf, "J. S. Bach: *Johannes Passion.*"

20. Metcalf, "J. S. Bach: *Johannes Passion.*"

21. Geck, *Johannes-Passion*, 16.

22. Glöckner, "Bach's *St. John Passion*," 70.

23. Michael Marissen, *Lutheranism, Anti-Judaism, and Bach's St. John Passion* (New York: Oxford University Press, 1998), 18–19.

3
St. Matthew Passion (BWV 244)

For many years it was thought that the *St. Matthew Passion* was first performed in the 1729 Good Friday afternoon service at St. Thomas Church in Leipzig. More recent research has suggested a performance already two years earlier: April 11, 1727. As a general rule, performances of large-scale Passions were performed in alternate years at St. Thomas and St. Nicholas (the other principal church in Leipzig). Subsequent performances of the *St. Matthew Passion* included the one in 1729, a performance in 1736 for which the work was revised and a new score and parts copied, and a further performance of the revised version around 1742. After that the work lay neglected for decades. Then, in 1829, one hundred years after its assumed first performance, Felix Mendelssohn revived the work in a performance that sparked the Bach revival of the nineteenth century.

Bach conceived the *St. Matthew Passion* in two sections, to be performed during the Good Friday Vespers service, with the first part preceding the sermon, the second part following it. In spite of its length—it is the longest of Bach's works—the Passion represented only part of the service, which also included hymns, prayers, a motet, and the sermon. The service must have lasted for several hours!

The text for the *St. Matthew Passion* is drawn from three sources:

1. the Gospel of Matthew, chapters 26 and 27 (according to Luther's translation, used intact),
2. verses from hymns (chorales) commonly used in Leipzig churches, and

3. devotional poetry commenting on the Passion narrative.

Most of these latter texts originate with a book of poetry corresponding to the services of the church year, called *Sammlung erbaulicher Gedanken über und auf die gewöhnlichen Sonn- und Feiertage*, published in 1725 in Leipzig by Christian Friedrich Henrici (pen name: Picander).

The *St. Matthew Passion* is an antiphonal work for double chorus and orchestra. The spatial element was apparently important to Bach's conception. The characters in the drama are represented by soloists, whom Bach assigned to particular choirs:

Choir I: Evangelist (tenor), Jesus (bass), Maid I (soprano), Maid II (soprano), Wife of Pilate (soprano), Judas (bass), Peter (bass), High Priest (bass), Pilate (bass), High Priests I and II (basses: see No. 41c)

Choir II: False Witness I (alto), False Witness II (tenor)

With the exception of Jesus, all characters presenting the Passion narrative sing in secco recitative—a style in which a solo vocal part with minimal accompaniment approximates the inflections of speech. For the most part, the Evangelist relates the story in an objective manner. Sometimes, however, he, too, reacts emotionally to the events. The story is told in all its details. The libretto omits nothing of the two biblical chapters (Matt. 26 and 27), including even those parts that might seem nonessential to the central Passion theme.

> [This] means certainly that [Bach] intended every textual nuance, however immaterial it may appear, to be clearly emphasized in shaping the Evangelist part. Scenes such as the story of the Potters' Field or the description of the women standing at the foot of the cross must not be treated as peripheral. In addition to the descriptive function of the Evangelist there are moments where Bach involves him directly in the unfolding events. . . . The theatrical nature of these highly dramatic moments—such as Jesus' arrest in Gethsemane or his interrogation by Pilate, in which the other solo characters become involved as well [call for the full exploitation of] Bach's rhythmic and dynamic subtleties.[1]

The story is presented at a leisurely pace. After each section of biblical narrative (sung by the Evangelist and other characters in the drama— including, at times, the crowd of bystanders, represented by one or both of the choruses) we hear several movements reflecting or commenting on the significance of the events just described: often a recitative in arioso (song-like) style follows, then an aria (a solo in which melodic characteristics predominate) transforms "the substance of the comment . . . into a prayer."[2]

Because of its more leisurely pace and more reflective character than the *St. John Passion*, the *St. Matthew Passion* is not as tightly knit as the former work. Nevertheless, it too is basically symmetrical in form, with the soprano aria, "Aus Liebe will mein Heiland sterben," serving as the centerpiece of the arch. A further element of unity is provided by the cyclical use of the "Passion Chorale" tune ("O Sacred Head Now Wounded"): Nos. 15 (21), 17 (23), 44 (53), 54 (63), and 62 (72). It is also hinted at in Nos. 23 (29), 35 (41), 39 (47), and 57 (66).

(*Note: For the convenience of readers using music scores employing the older numbering system rather than the one used in the new collected edition, movement numbers are given here according to both schemes whenever they differ.*[3])

Part I

The large-scale, chorale-based opening movement presents the listener with several levels of thought: on the most immediate level we hear an invitation to follow Christ on the path to his crucifixion ("Sehet ihn aus Lieb und Huld Holz zum Kreuz selber tragen"). Then, to explore the significance of the events, Bach presents a dialogue between the two choruses, which serves "as a conversation between the Passion account and the hearing congregation."[4] The accompanying chorale ("O Lamm Gottes, unschuldig") presents a third layer. This hymn is essentially a German setting of the liturgical Agnus Dei. With it we encounter the ecclesiastical level of "liturgically objectified confession," which reaches "its intended spiritual climax" with the words "Erbarm dich unser, o Jesu." The very opening words ("Kommt, ihr Töchter") are "derived in thought and content from the Song of Solomon" and introduce that plane of the work that is "of most personal expression and immediacy of expression."[5]

From a tonal perspective it is interesting to note that, while the movement as a whole is in a minor key, the chorale is in G major. That this was technically possible suggests that Bach advised Picander with regard to the libretto.

The most notable rhythmic feature of the movement is its meter: the lilting 12/8 pattern of the siciliano, a baroque dance with pastoral associations. Accentuated by a throbbing bass line (which does not move from its initial pitch for the first ten measures) the siciliano rhythm underscores the central theme of the work: it is the account of the sacrifice of the Lamb of God, the "Agnus Dei."

1. Double Chorus and Chorale

Kommt, ihr Töchter, helft mir klagen,	Come, you daughters, help me lament,
sehet . . .	see . . .
Wen?	Whom?
. . . den Bräutigam,	. . . the bridegroom,
seht ihn . . .	see him . . .
Wie?	How?
. . . als wie ein Lamm!	. . . as a Lamb.
Sehet . . .	See . . .
Was?	What?
. . . seht die Geduld,	. . . see his patience.
seht . . .	Look . . .
Wohin?	Where?
. . . auf unsre Schuld;	. . . upon our guilt;
sehet ihn aus Lieb und Huld	see how, out of love and grace,
Holz zum Kreuze selber tragen!	he himself bears the wood for a cross!

O Lamm Gottes, unschuldig	O Lamb of God, innocent,
am Stamm des Kreuzes geschlachtet,	slaughtered upon the cross's beam,
allzeit erfunden geduldig,	always found forbearing,
wiewohl du warest verachtet.	although treated with scorn.
All Sünd hast du getragen,	All sin you have borne,
sonst müßten wir verzagen.	else would we despair.
Erbarm dich unser, o Jesu!	Have mercy on us, O Jesus!

The Evangelist begins the story with Christ's own prophecy of his impending crucifixion. When Jesus sings, his words are accompanied by a "halo" of strings. The chorale that follows represents the first response of the listeners to the story: their agitation and anguish are reflected in Bach's choice of a high key and intense harmonies.

2. Recitative (Evangelist and Jesus)

Da Jesus diese Rede vollendet hatte,	When Jesus had finished this discourse,
sprach er zu seinen Jüngern: Ihr wisset,	he said to his disciples, "You know that
daß nach zweien Tagen Ostern wird, und	the Passover is two days hence, and the
des Menschen Sohn wird überantwortet	Son of Man will be delivered up to be
werden, daß er gekreuziget werde.	crucified."

3. Chorale

Herzliebster Jesu,	Beloved Jesus,
was hast du verbrochen,	what is your trespassing,
daß man ein solch scharf Urteil	that such a cruel judgment
hat gesprochen?	has been spoken?
Was ist die Schuld,	What is the guilt,

**in was für Missetaten
bist du geraten?**

into what sort of transgressions
have you fallen?

4a. (4.) Recitative (Evangelist)
*Da versammleten sich die Hohenpriester
und Schriftgelehrten und die Ältesten im
Volk in den Palast des Hohenpriesters,
der da hieß Kaiphas; und hielten Rat,
wie sie Jesum mit Listen griffen und töteten. Sie sprachen aber:*

Then the high priests and the scribes
and the elders of the people assembled
in the palace of the high priest, whose
name was Caiaphas, and counseled
there how they might take Jesus by craft
and put him to death. But they said:

As the religious leaders, plotting against Jesus, consider the possibility of
an uproar among the people, we can hear the excited tumult of the crowds
coming into the city to celebrate the Passover.

4b. (5.) Chorus
*Ja nicht auf das Fest, auf daß nicht ein
Aufruhr werde im Volk.*

But not during the feast, lest an uproar
occur among the people.

Meanwhile, at the home of a disciple called "Simon the leper," a woman
(whom a parallel Gospel account identifies as Mary) anoints Jesus' head
with perfume.

4c. (6.) Recitative (Evangelist)
*Da nun Jesus war zu Bethanien, im
Hause Simonis des Aussätzigen, trat zu
ihm ein Weib, die hatte ein Glas mit
köstlichem Wasser und goß es auf sein
Haupt, da er zu Tische saß. Da das
seine Jünger sahen, wurden sie unwillig
und sprachen:*

Now when Jesus was in Bethany, in the
house of Simon the Leper, a woman
came to him; she had a bottle of precious liquid, which she poured on his
head as he sat at table. When His disciples saw it they became indignant and
said:

We hear the disciples' irritation and indignation as they chatter amongst
one another. That Bach also viewed them as inflexibly self-righteous is
evidenced by his use of strict imitation.

4d. (7.) Chorus
*Wozu dienet dieser Unrat? Dieses Was-
ser hätte mögen teuer verkauft, und den
Armen gegeben werden.*

What is the point of this waste? This
liquid could have been sold for a goodly
sum, and the proceeds given to the poor.

In contrast to the disciples, whose disgusted response reveals a short-
sighted and miserly mind-set, Jesus affirms the woman. He notes the
symbolic significance of her action in view of his impending burial, which
Bach portrays musically with a descending sighing motive.

4e. (8.) Recitative (Evangelist and Jesus)

Da das Jesus merkete, sprach er zu ihnen: Was bekümmert ihr das Weib? Sie hat ein gut Werk an mir getan. Ihr habet allezeit Armen bei euch, mich aber habt ihr nicht allezeit. Daß sie dies Wasser hat auf meinen Leib gegossen, hat sie getan, daß man mich begraben wird. Wahrlich, ich sage euch: Wo dies Evangelium geprediget wird in der ganzen Welt, da wird man auch sagen zu ihrem Gedächtnis, was sie getan hat.	When Jesus noticed this, he said to them, "Why do you bother the woman? She has done me a good deed. You will always have the poor among you, but you will not always have me. She has poured this liquid on my body for my burial. Truly, I say to you, wherever this Gospel shall be preached throughout the whole world, the thing this woman has done shall be spoken in her remembrance."

A second recitative, reflective rather than narrative in nature, follows Jesus' response. Here the alto soloist, representing the individual Christian believer, is accompanied musically by two transverse flutes, whose shared motive depicts the textual ideas of costly perfume and tears. In its chromatic depiction of weeping, the singer's line covers all twelve tones of the octave in the course of seven measures, a phenomenon not uncommon in Bach's settings of texts describing repentance and remorse.

5. (9.) Alto Recitative

Du lieber Heiland du,	Dearest Savior,
wenn deine Jünger töricht streiten,	if your disciples quarrel foolishly
daß dieses fromme Weib	because this pious woman
mit Salben deinen Leib	with ointment
zum Grabe will bereiten,	would prepare your body for burial,
so lasse mir inzwischen zu,	then let me meanwhile
von meiner Augen Tränenflüssen	pour a teary water
ein Wasser	from my streaming eyes
auf dein Haupt zu gießen!	upon your head!

The alto continues with these sentiments in the following aria. The literary concepts of consciousness of sin, penance, and remorse are worked out in chromatic lines and harmonies set to a moderately paced dance rhythm, giving the movement a resigned, benumbed quality. A sighing-weeping figure ties this movement to the preceding one; in the middle section, where the text speaks of teardrops, the aural imagery is made explicit.

6. (10.) Alto Aria

Buß und Reu	Penitence and remorse
knirscht das Sündenherz entzwei;	gnash the sinful heart asunder,
daß die Tropfen meiner Zähren	so that the teardrops of my weeping
angenehme Spezerei,	become pleasant spices for you,
treuer Jesu, dir gebären.	dear Jesus.

In complete contrast, we now encounter Judas, the epitome of the unfaithful disciple.

7. (11.) Recitative (Evangelist and Judas)

Da ging hin der Zwölfen einer mit Namen Judas Ischarioth zu den Hohenpriestern und sprach: Was wollt ihr mir geben? Ich will ihn euch verraten. Und sie boten ihm dreißig Silberlinge. Und von dem an suchte er Gelegenheit, daß er ihn verriete.

Then one of the twelve, whose name was Judas Iscariot, went to the high priests and said, "What will you give me? I will betray him to you." And they offered him thirty pieces of silver. And from then on he sought opportunity to betray him.

The droplet-sobbing motive returns in the soprano aria, "Blute nur." This aria is linked to the former movement also in its quasi-dance rhythm and its flute instrumentation. Noteworthy here is the fact that the first flute always doubles the soprano voice whenever it is present.

8. (12.) Soprano Aria

Blute nur, du liebes Herz!
Ach! ein Kind, das du erzogen,
das an deiner Brust gesogen,
droht den Pfleger zu ermorden,
denn es ist zur Schlange worden.

Bleed, beloved heart!
Ah, a child whom you raised,
that suckled at your breast,
threatens to murder the nourisher,
because it has turned into a serpent.

The narrator now begins to relate the events of the Feast of Unleavened Bread, an annual celebration of Israel's deliverance from Egypt that began with the Passover meal on the fourteenth day of the first month (Abib = Nisan) and continued for seven days.[6]

9a. (13.) Recitative (Evangelist)

Aber am ersten Tage der süßen Brot traten die Jünger zu Jesu, und sprachen zu ihm:

Now on the first day of unleavened bread the disciples came to Jesus, and said to him:

The following chorus is relatively brief and straightforward, with melodic lines that meander in opposite directions suggesting the "serene, uncomplicated deportment of the disciples"[7] as they wonder where to have the ceremonial meal with Jesus. The fact that Bach employed exactly fourteen measures for the disciples' question (recitative and chorus) suggests that he may have wanted to symbolize the fact that it was the fourteenth day of the month.

9b. (14.) Chorus

Wo willst du, daß wir dir bereiten, das Osterlamm zu essen?"

Where would you have us make preparations for you to eat the Passover lamb?

9c, d, e. (15.) Recitative (Evangelist and
Jesus) and **Chorus**
*Er sprach: Gehet hin in die Stadt zu
einem und sprecht zu ihm: Der Meister
läßt dir sagen: Meine Zeit ist hier, ich will
bei dir die Ostern halten mit meinen
Jüngern. Und die Jünger täten, wie ihnen
Jesus befohlen hatte, und bereiteten das
Osterlamm.
Und am Abend satzte er sich zu Tische
mit den Zwölfen. Und da sie aßen,
sprach er: Wahrlich, ich sage euch:
Einer unter euch wird mich verraten. Und
sie wurden sehr betrübt und huben an,
ein jeglicher unter ihnen, und sagten zu
ihm: Herr, bin ichs?*

He said, "Go into the city, to a certain
man, and say to him: The master bids us
tell you, 'My time has come; I wish to
hold the Passover at your house with my
disciples.'" And the disciples did as Jesus had instructed them and prepared
the Passover lamb.
And in the evening he seated himself at
table with the twelve. And as they ate, he
said, "Truly I say to you, one of you will
betray me." And they were deeply trou-
bled, and each one began to say to him,
"Lord, is it I?"

During the course of the meal Jesus abruptly states that one of them will
betray him. At these words the music unexpectedly veers to C minor,
instead of the prepared C major. The disciples show agitated disbelief,
asking, "Lord, is it I?" Before Jesus can answer, the congregation responds, admitting its guilt.

10. (16.) Chorale
**Ich bins, ich sollte büßen,
an Händen und an Füßen
gebunden in der Höll.
Die Geißeln und die Banden
und was du ausgestanden,
das hat verdienet meine Seel.**

'Tis I who should atone,
bound hand and foot
in hell.
The scourges and the shackles,
and all that you endured
my soul has deserved.

Despite the disciples' agitation, Jesus' response is calm, his manner
serene, even when Judas echoes the others' question hypocritically. As he
plays the host, Jesus offers a lyrical reinterpretation of the symbolic
meaning of the bread and wine: they are henceforth to be understood as
the elements of a new covenant. At this point in Bach's musical setting,
recitative gives way to arioso, a more song-like style in which the rhythm
is regular and the vocal part somewhat melismatic (i.e., text syllables are
given two or more notes each).

11. (17.) Recitative (Evangelist, Jesus,
Judas)
*Er antwortete und sprach: Der mit der
Hand mit mir in die Schüssel tauchet, der
wird mich verraten. Des Menschen Sohn
gehet zwar dahin, wie von ihm geschrieben stehet: doch wehe dem Menschen,
durch welchen des Menschen Sohn*

He answered and said, "He who dips his
hand with me in the dish will betray me.
The Son of Man indeed goes his forth,
as has been written of him, but woe to
the person by whom the Son of Man

verraten wird! Es wäre ihm besser, daß derselbige Mensch noch nie geboren wäre.
Da antwortete Judas, der ihn verriet, und sprach: Bin ichs Rabbi? Er sprach zu ihm: Du sagests.
Da sie aber aßen, nahm Jesus das Brot, dankete, und brachs, und gabs den Jüngern und sprach: Nehmet, esset, das ist mein Leib. Und er nahm den Kelch und dankete, gab ihnen den und sprach: Trinket alle daraus; das ist mein Blut des neuen Testaments, welches vergossen wird für viele zur Vergebung der Sünden. Ich sage euch: Ich werde von nun an nicht mehr von diesem Gewächs des Weinstocks trinken bis an den Tag, da ichs neu trinken werde mit euch in meines Vaters Reich.

shall be betrayed! For him it were better if he had never been born."
Then Judas, who betrayed him, answered and said, "Is it I, rabbi?" He said to him, "You are saying it."
But as they were eating, Jesus took the bread, gave thanks, broke it, and gave it to the disciples and said, "Take, eat, this is my body." And he took the cup, and giving thanks, he gave it to them saying, "Drink of it, all of you; this is my blood of the new testament, which is being shed for many, in remission of sins. I say to you, from henceforth I will no longer drink of this fruit of the vine, until the day when I drink it anew with you in my Father's kingdom."

An accompanied recitative of great emotion and expression follows. The individual disciple (who also represents the contemporary believer) is torn with sadness at the prospect of Jesus' departure yet is gradually comforted by the pledge of the new covenant made in the Lord's Supper. The pathos of the scene is underscored by two oboes d'amore playing circular sixteenth-note triplet figures in parallel thirds and sixths, and a bass that moves chromatically in throbbing eighth notes. The movement ends with an allusion to the parallel account in the Gospel of John: "Now before the feast of the Passover, when Jesus knew that his hour had come to depart out of this world to the Father, having loved his own who were in the world, he loved them to the end."[8]

12. (18.) Soprano Recitative

Wiewohl mein Herz
in Tränen schwimmt,
daß Jesus von mir Abschied nimmt,
so macht mich doch
sein Testament erfreut:
Sein Fleisch und Blut, o Kostbarkeit,
vermacht er mir in meine Hände.
Wie er es auf der Welt mit denen Seinen
nicht böse können meinen,
so liebt er sie bis an das Ende.

Although my heart
is awash with tears
because Jesus takes leave of me,
yet I am gladdened
by his testament:
his flesh and blood, O precious gift,
he bequeaths into my hands.
As he can never be ill disposed
toward those who are his own on earth,
so he loves them to the end.

Recalling musical motives from the Last Supper scene in the oboes d'amore and bass instruments, the soprano aria contemplates the Eucharistic elements of Christ's body and blood in a playful prayer addressed to the heavenly bridegroom.

13. (19.) Soprano Aria

Ich will dir mein Herze schenken,	I want to give you my heart,
senke dich, mein Heil, hinein.	sink into it, O my salvation.
Ich will mich in dir versenken;	I want to submerge myself in you;
ist dir gleich die Welt zu klein,	though this earth be too small for you,
ei so sollst du mir allein	you alone shall be
mehr als Welt und Himmel sein.	more than earth and heaven to me.

After two movements of introspection, the narrator resumes the story. The recitative is rich with text-painting: rising lines in the string parts portray the group's ascent of the Mount of Olives as well as Jesus' coming resurrection, and rapid staccato notes accompany Jesus' warning that the disciples will abandon him, scattering like sheep.

14. (20.) Recitative (Evangelist and Jesus)

Und da sie den Lobgesang gesprochen hatten, gingen sie hinaus an den Ölberg. Da sprach Jesus zu ihnen: In dieser Nacht werdet ihr euch alle ärgern an mir. Denn es stehet geschrieben: Ich werde den Hirten schlagen, und die Schafe der Herde werden sich zerstreuen. Wenn ich aber auferstehe, will ich vor euch hingehen in Galiläam.	And when they had said the hymn of praise, they went out to the Mount of Olives. Then Jesus said to them, "This night you shall all be offended because of me. For it is written, 'I will smite the shepherd, and the sheep of the flock shall be scattered.' But when I rise again, I will go before you into Galilee."

Responding to Jesus' prediction that all will abandon him as sheep abandon a shepherd who has been struck down, the congregation sings a prayer to Christ the Good Shepherd. The tune is that of the "Passion Chorale;" it appears another four times in the course of the work.

15. (21.) Chorale

Erkenne mich, mein Hüter,	Acknowledge me, my guardian,
mein Hirte nimm, mich an!	my shepherd, accept me!
Von dir, Quell aller Güter,	From you, O source of every blessing,
ist mir viel Guts getan.	much good has come to me.
Dein Mund hat mich gelabet	Your mouth has nourished me
mit Milch und süßer Kost,	with milk and sweet fare;
dein Geist hat mich begabet	your spirit has brought me
mit mancher Himmelslust.	many a heavenly pleasure.

16. (22.) Recitative (Evangelist, Peter, Jesus)

Petrus aber antwortete und sprach zu ihm: Wenn sie auch alle sich an dir ärgerten, so will ich doch mich nimmermehr ärgern. Jesus sprach zu ihm: Wahrlich, ich sage dir: in dieser Nacht, ehe der Hahn krähet, wirst du mich dreimal verleugnen. Petrus sprach zu ihm: Und wenn ich mit dir sterben müßte, so will ich dich nicht verleugnen. Desgleichen sagten auch alle Jünger.

But Peter answered and said to him, "Though all be offended because of you, yet will I, Lord, never be offended." Jesus said to him, "Truly I say to you, this very night, before the cock crows, you will deny me three times." Peter said to him, "Though I should have to die with you, I will never deny you." And all the disciples said likewise.

After Peter's assertion that he will never deny Christ, the congregation asserts its own commitment to faithfulness in a repetition of the hymn just sung—but now in a key one semitone lower, giving a sense of growing uncertainty and even foreboding. This is the second appearance of the "Passion Chorale."

17. (23.) Chorale
Ich will hier bei dir stehen;
verachte mich doch nicht!
Von dir will ich nicht gehen,
wenn dir dein Herze bricht.
Wenn dein Herz wird erblassen
im letzen Todesstoß,
alsdenn will ich dich fassen
in meinen Arm und Schoß.

I want to stand here by you,
do not despise me!
I will not leave you
when your heart is broken.
When your heart turns pale
in the last throes of death,
then I will hold you
in my arms and bosom.

As Jesus enters the spiritual and mental agonies of Gethsemane, the Evangelist can no longer remain dispassionate. He abandons syllabic presentation for a more heartfelt melismatic one on the words, "[he] . . . began to grieve and despair." When Jesus sings, "My soul is grieved to the point of death," the depth of his emotional distress is revealed in the strings, which play a "quaking" figure of pulsed eighth notes.

18. (24.) Recitative (Evangelist and Jesus)

Da kam Jesus mit ihnen zu einem Hofe, der hieß Gethsemane, und sprach zu seinen Jüngern: Setzet euch hie, bis daß ich dort hingehe, und bete. Und nahm zu sich Petrum und die zween Söhne Zebedäi, und fing an zu trauern und zu zagen. Da sprach Jesus zu ihnen: Meine Seele ist betrübt bis in den Tod, bleibet hie und wachet mit mir.

Then Jesus came with them to a place called Gethsemane, and said to his disciples, "Sit here while I go yonder and pray." And he took with him Peter and the two sons of Zebedee, and began to grieve and despair. Then Jesus said to them, "My soul is grieved to the point of death; stay here and keep watch with me."

While the tenor soloist and orchestra of Choir I agonize over Christ's predicament in animated musical gestures (e.g., the "quaking" figure of the bass instruments), Choir II recognizes its own guilt in a somber chorale. Because Bach assigned the next two solos to the tenor of Choir I (whether or not they are sung by the Evangelist in modern performance) we are left with the impression that the narrator has continued to sing, abandoning his objective role for a more personal involvement. The hymn sung by Choir II amplifies the text of the recitative—not vice versa, which is more usually the case in movements combining recitative and chorale.

19. (25.) Tenor Recitative and Chorus
(Chorale)

O Schmerz!	O anguish!
hier zittert das gequälte Herz;	Here the tormented heart trembles;
wie sinkt es hin,	how it sinks,
wie bleicht sein Angesicht!	how his face pales!
Was ist die Ursach	What is the cause
aller solcher Plagen?	of all these torments?
Der Richter führt ihn vor Gericht.	The judge leads him to judgment.
Da ist kein Trost, kein Helfer nicht.	There is no comfort, no one to help.
Ach, meine Sünden	Ah, my sins
haben dich geschlagen;	have struck you;
Er leidet alle Höllenqualen,	He suffers all the torments of hell,
er soll vor fremden Raub bezahlen.	he must pay for others' plundering.
ich, ach Herr Jesu,	Ah, Lord Jesus
habe dies verschuldet,	mine is the blame,
was du erduldet.	for what you have suffered.
Ach, könnte meine Liebe dir,	Ah, if only my love for you,
mein Heil, dein Zittern und dein Zagen	my Savior, could diminish or help bear
vermindern oder helfen tragen,	your trembling and your fear,
wie gerne blieb ich hier!	how gladly I would stay here!

The tenor aria commences with the opposing concepts of "waking" and "sleeping." The soloist states his determination to keep watch through the night with his Lord, while the chorus sings that by keeping vigil with Christ "sins fall asleep." Bach accentuates the antithesis of the implied theological paradox with various musical means including held notes to suggest "determined waking" and two-note sighing figures and a continuously soft choral dynamic to portray "falling asleep."

**20. (26.) Tenor Aria and Chorus (Cho-
rale text)**

Ich will bei meinem Jesu wachen,	I will keep watch with my Jesus,
So schlafen unsre Sünden ein.	Then all our sins will fall asleep.
Meinen Tod büßet seine Seelennot;	His soul's distress atones my death;
sein Trauren machet mich voll Freuden.	his sorrow brings me gladness.
Drum muß uns	Thus must
sein verdienstlich Leiden	his meritorious suffering for us
recht bitter und doch süße sein.	be bitter and yet sweet.

21. (27.) Recitative (Evangelist and Jesus)

Und ging hin ein wenig, fiel nieder auf	And he went a little farther, fell down
sein Angesicht und betete und sprach:	upon his face and prayed, and said, "My
Mein Vater, ists möglich, so gehe dieser	Father if it is possible, let this cup pass
Kelch von mir; doch nicht wie ich will,	from me, yet not as I will, but as you will."
sondern wie du willt.	

The theological paradox is explored further by the bass soloist: Christ's willingness to bow to his Father's will (depicted by descending arpeggios in the strings) raises believers from their fallen state to a renewed state of grace with the Father (here the musical figure is suddenly inverted).

22. (28.) Bass Recitative

Der Heiland fällt	The Savior falls down
vor seinem Vater nieder;	before his Father;
dadurch erhebt er mich und alle	thereby he raises me, and all,
von unserm Falle	from our fall
hinauf zu Gottes Gnade wieder.	up to God's grace again.
Er ist bereit, den Kelch,	He is prepared
des Todes Bitterkeit zu trinken,	to drink the bitter cup of death,
in welchen Sünden dieser Welt	into which the sins of this world
gegossen sind	have been poured,
und häßlich stinken,	and which stink awfully,
weil es dem lieben Gott gefällt.	because our dear God has willed it so.

In the bass aria that follows, the cross and cup of Christ's suffering reappear as symbols of submission as the believer expresses willingness to emulate Jesus' example by embracing them. Perhaps not coincidentally Bach sets these words with a chromatic melodic figure that spells his name in reverse: H-C-A-B (according to German nomenclature B is B-flat; H is B-natural). Twice Bach also subtly incorporates the opening notes of the chorale "O Sacred Head" into the instrumental bass line.

23. (29.) Bass Aria

Gerne will ich mich bequemen,	Gladly will I submit myself
Kreuz und Becher anzunehmen,	to taking up cross and cup,
trink ich doch dem Heiland nach.	drinking as my Savior did.
Denn sein Mund,	For his mouth,
der mit Milch und Honig fließet,	with milk and honey flowing,
hat den Grund	have sweetened the dregs
und des Leidens herbe Schmach	and bitter disgrace of suffering
durch den ersten Trunk versüßet.	by taking the first drink.

24. (30.) Recitative (Evangelist and Jesus)

Und er kam zu seinen Jüngern und fand sie schlafend und sprach zu ihnen: Könnet ihr denn nicht eine Stunde mir mir wachen? Wachet und betet, daß ihr nicht in Anfechtung fallet! Der Geist ist willig, aber das Fleisch ist schwach. Zum andernmal ging er hin, betete und sprach: Mein Vater, ists nicht möglich, daß dieser Kelch von mir gehe, ich trinke ihn denn, so geschehe dein Wille.

And he came to his disciples and found them sleeping and said to them, "Can you not keep watch with me for one hour? Watch and pray that you may not fall into temptation! The spirit is willing but the flesh is weak." He went away again, prayed, and said, "My Father, if it is not possible that this cup pass from me unless I drink it, then let your will be done."

Upon Jesus' repeated words of submission, the choruses take up his words and generalize them.

25. (31.) Chorale

Was mein Gott will,	Whatever my God wills,
das gscheh allzeit,	may that always come to pass;
sein Will, der ist der beste.	his will is best.
Zu helfen den' er ist bereit,	He is ready to help those
die an ihn gläuben feste.	who believe firmly in him.
Er hilft aus Not,	He delivers from trouble,
der fromme Gott,	this good God,
und züchtiget mit Maßen.	and chastens in moderation.
Wer Gott vertraut,	Whoever trusts in God,
fest auf ihn baut,	and builds on him firmly,
den will er nicht verlassen.	will not be forsaken by him.

The next events unfold rapidly. To maintain dramatic momentum the librettist does not interrupt the biblical account again until after Jesus' betrayal and capture. As Jesus announces the imminent event, more and more sharped notes appear in the music, perhaps intended by Bach to symbolize the coming crucifixion (in German the sharp sign is called "Kreuz," which is also the word for "cross").

26. (32.) Recitative (Evangelist, Jesus, Judas)

Und er kam und fand sie aber schlafend, und ihre Augen waren voll Schlafs. Und er ließ sie und ging abermal hin und betete zum drittenmal und redete dieselbigen Worte. Da kam er zu seinen Jüngern und sprach zu ihnen: Ach! wollt ihr nun schlafen und ruhen? Siehe, die Stunde ist hie, daß des Menschen Sohn in der Sünder Hände überantwortet wird. Stehet auf, lasset uns gehen; siehe, er ist da, der mich verrät. Und als er noch redete, siehe, da kam Judas, der Zwölfen einer, und mit ihm eine große Schar mit Schwertern und mit Stangen von den Hohenpriestern und Ältesten des Volks. Und der Verräter hatte ihnen ein Zeichen gegeben und gesagt: "Welchen ich küssen werde, der ists, den greifet!" Und alsbald trat er zu Jesu und sprach: Gegrüßet seist du, Rabbi! und küssete ihn. Jesus aber sprach zu ihm: Mein Freund! warum bist du kommen? Da traten sie hinzu und legten die Hände an Jesum und griffen ihn.

And he came and found them sleeping, and their eyes were heavy with sleep. And he left them, and went again, and prayed for the third time, saying the same words. Then he came to his disciples and said to them, "Ah, do you now want to sleep and rest? See, the hour is here for the Son of Man to be delivered into the hands of sinners. Rise up, let us be going; see, the one who betrays me is here." And as he was still speaking, lo, Judas, who was one of the twelve, came, and with him a large crowd, with swords and with staves, from the high priests and the elders of the people. And the traitor had given them a sign saying, "The one whom I shall kiss is he, seize him!" And he immediately came to Jesus and said, "Hail, Rabbi!" and kissed him. But Jesus said to him, "My friend, why have you come?" Then they came and laid their hands on Jesus and seized him."

After Jesus is betrayed and captured, the soloists look on in disbelief, while the chorus interjects with outbursts protesting his capture. The physical act of leading Jesus away is reflected in the imitative writing of the vocal and wind parts, one line imitating the other at a time interval of one or two measures. The dazed reaction of the soloists is reflected in Bach's musical texture, which lacks the usual foundation of a bass line. The movement concludes with a fiery call for thunder and lightning to destroy the betrayer. The question is not simply rhetorical: a grand pause signals that the sympathetic bystanders expect a response. When heaven is silent, the call to avenge the injustice is extended to the very abyss of hell. Perhaps to show the ultimately positive outcome of these events, Bach sets the final word, "Blut," with a radiant E major chord.

27a, b. (33.) Soprano and Alto Duet and Chorus

So ist mein Jesus nun gefangen.
    Lasst ihn, haltet, bindet nicht!
Mond und Licht
ist vor Schmerzen untergangen,
weil mein Jesus ist gefangen.
    Lasst ihn, haltet, bindet nicht!

Thus my Jesus has now been taken.
    Leave him! Halt! Do not bind him!
Moon and light
have set in anguish,
because my Jesus has been taken.
    Leave him! Halt! Do not bind him!

Sie führen ihn, er ist gebunden.	They lead him; he is bound.
Sind Blitze, sind Donner	Have lightning, have thunder
in Wolken verschwunden?	vanished in the clouds?
Eröffne den feurigen Abgrund,	Open your fiery abyss,
o Hölle,	O hell,
zertrümmre, verderbe,	crush, destroy,
verschlinge, zerschelle,	devour, shatter,
mit plötzlicher Wut	with sudden rage,
den falschen Verräter,	the false-hearted traitor,
das mördrische Blut!	the murderous blood!

One of the disciples (listeners in Bach's day would have known from a parallel Gospel account that it was the always impetuous Peter) decides to take action. But Jesus remains calm and submissive, and the disciples flee in confusion.

28. (34.) Recitative (Evangelist and Jesus)

Und siehe, einer aus denen, die mit Jesu waren, rekkete die Hand aus, und schlug des Hohenpriesters Knecht und hieb ihm ein Ohr ab. Da sprach Jesus zu ihm: Stekke dein Schwert an seinen Ort; denn wer das Schwert nimmt, der soll durchs Schwert umkommen. Oder meinest du, daß ich nicht könnte meinen Vater bitten, daß er mir zuschickte mehr denn zwölf Legion Engel? Wie würde aber die Schrift erfüllet? Es muß also gehen.	And lo, one of those who were with Jesus, stretched out his hand and struck the high priest's servant, cutting off his ear. Then Jesus said to him, "Put your sword in its place, for whoever takes the sword will perish by the sword. Or do you think that I could not ask my Father to send me more than twelve legions of angels? But how, then, would scripture be fulfilled? It must be so."
Zu der Stund sprach Jesus zu den Scharen: Ihr seid ausgegangen, als zu einem Mörder, mit Schwerten und mit Stangen, mich zu fahen; bin ich doch täglich bei euch gesessen und habe gelehret im Tempel, und ihr habt mich nicht gegriffen. Aber das ist alles geschehen, daß erfüllet würden die Schriften der Propheten. Da verließen ihn alle Jünger, und flohen.	At that hour Jesus said to the crowds, "You have gone out as if against a murderer, with swords and with staves, to catch me; yet I sat with you daily and taught in the temple, and you did not lay hold of me." But all of this has occurred to fulfill the scriptures of the prophets." Then all the disciples forsook him and fled.

To close Part I Bach chose to reuse a chorale-based movement from the second version of his *St. John Passion*. This complex hymn setting for chorus and orchestra balances the opening movement of the work. Both are calls to lamentation. Here it is a universal call to repentance in view of the voluntary incarnation and Passion of Christ, a fitting bridge to the sermon, which occurred at this point in Bach's day. The primary musical gesture is a sighing figure, which appears in all accompanying parts while the soprano presents the hymn tune.

29. (35.) Chorus

O Mensch, bewein dein Sünde groß,	O man, your grievous sin bemoan,
darum Christus seins Vaters Schoß	for which Christ left his Father's bosom
äußert und kam auf Erden;	and came to earth.
von einer Jungfrau rein und zart	Of a virgin pure and tender,
für uns er hie geboren ward,	he was born for us here;
er wollt der Mittler werden.	he wanted to become the mediator.
Den Toten er das Leben gab	To the dead he gave life,
und legt darbei all Krankheit ab,	and therewith put away all sickness,
bis sich die Zeit herdrange,	until the time appointed,
daß er für uns geopfert würd,	when he would be sacrificed for us,
trüg unsrer Sünden schwere Bürd	bearing our sins' heavy burden
wohl an dem Kreuze lange.	on the cross.

Part II

With Jesus having been captured, Part II begins with a movement of great inner textual contrast: while the alto soloist of Chorus I agonizes over the capture of her closest friend, utilizing the rhythm of the sarabande (a dance of moderate speed in triple meter, characterized by a secondary accent on beat 2), onlookers (played by Choir II) ask innocently where her lover has gone, using words from the Song of Solomon and the lighter rhythm of the courtly minuet.

30. (36.) Alto Aria and Chorus

Ach, nun ist mein Jesus hin!	Ah, now my Jesus is gone!
Wo ist denn	Where then
dein Freund hingegangen,	has your beloved gone,
o du Schönste unter den Weibern?	O fairest among women?
Ist es möglich, kann ich schauen?	Is it possible, can I see it?
Wo hat sich	Where has
dein Freund hingewandt?	your beloved taken himself?
Ach! mein Lamm in Tigerklauen,	Ah, my lamb in tiger's claws!
Ach! wo ist mein Jesus hin?	Ah, where has my Jesus gone?
So wollen wir	We will go
mit dir ihn suchen.	with you to seek him.
Ach! was soll ich der Seele sagen,	Ah, what shall I say to the soul
wenn sie mich wird ängstlich fragen?	when it asks me anxiously?
Ach! wo ist mein Jesus hin?	Ah, where has my Jesus gone?

The next scene shows Jesus before the religious high council. His enemies try to find cause to sentence him to death but find none. Bach sets the scene simply, as a minimally accompanied recitative that modulates downward from E minor to D major.

82   Chapter 3

31. (37.) Recitative (Evangelist)

Die aber Jesum gegriffen hatten, führe-
ten ihn zu dem Hohenpriester Kaiphas,
dahin die Schriftgelehrten und Ältesten
sich versammelt hatten. Petrus aber
folgete ihm nach von ferne bis in den
Palast des Hohenpriesters und ging hin-
ein und satzte sich bei die Knechte, auf
daß er sähe, wo es hinaus wollte. Die
Hohenpriester aber und Ältesten und der
ganze Rat suchten falsche Zeugnis
wider Jesum, auf daß sie ihn töteten,
und funden keines.

But those who had apprehended Jesus
led him to the high priest, Caiaphas,
where the scribes and elders had assembled. But Peter followed him at a
distance as far as the high priest's palace, went inside, and sat down with the
officers, to see how all this would end.
The high priests, however, and the elders, and the entire council sought false
testimony against Jesus, so that they
could put him to death, but they found
none.

In the following chorale the chorus contemplates its own experiences with
treacherous foes. The range is high for a hymn, and the harmony intense.

32. (38.) Chorale

Mir hat die Welt trüglich gericht'
mit Lügen und mit falschem Gdicht,
viel Netz und heimlich Strikke.
Herr, nimm mein wahr
in dieser Gfahr,
bhüt mich für falschen Tükken.

The world has judged me falsely
with lies and deceitful inventions,
many traps and secret snares.
Lord, protect me
in this danger,
shelter me from deceitful wiles.

Finally the collaborators remember a statement of Jesus that can be used
against him, and bring forward two prepared witnesses. In contrast to the
poised demeanor of Jesus, the two seem flustered, singing in a much
higher range, and at a much quicker pace. Mosaic law required accusers
to present at least two witnesses,[9] and now the second man, in his excitement, interrupts his partner with his own statement, which is almost note-
for-note identical, suggesting it has been rehearsed beforehand.

33. (39.) Recitative (Evangelist, False
Witnesses, High Priest)

Und wiewohl viel falsche Zeugen herzu-
traten, funden sie doch keins. Zuletzt
traten herzu zween falsche Zeugen und
sprachen: Er hat gesagt: Ich kann den
Tempel Gottes abbrechen und in dreien
Tagen denselben bauen. Und der Hohe-
priester stund auf und sprach zu ihm:
Antwortest du nichts zu dem, das diese
wider dich zeugen? Aber Jesus schwieg
stille.

And although many false witnesses
came forward, they still found none. Finally two false witnesses came forward
and said, "He has said, 'I can destroy the
temple of God and rebuild the same in
three days.'" And the high priest stood up
and said to him, "Will you not answer any
of the testimony these are bringing
against you?" But Jesus remained silent.

A recitative for tenor follows. The accompanying instruments play
repeated chords in monotonous fashion, suggesting Jesus' determination

to suffer in silence. The exact number of chords in ten measures is 39—perhaps intended as a numerical allusion to Psalm 39:10: "I will bridle my mouth, so long as the wicked are in my presence. . . . I was dumb and silent."

34. (40.) Tenor Recitative

Mein Jesus schweigt	My Jesus does not answer
zu falschen Lügen stille,	the false lies,
um uns damit zu zeigen,	to show us thereby
daß sein Erbarmens voller Wille	that, full of mercy, his will
vor uns zum Leiden sei geneigt,	is surrendered to suffer for us,
und daß wir in dergleichen Pein	and that we, when in similar distress,
ihm sollen ähnlich sein	are to be like him,
und in Verfolgung stille schweigen.	and remain silent in persecution.

The tenor aria is built on two contrasting musical ideas, which arise directly from the literary images in the first text phrase. A jabbing bass line (which is underscored by the addition of a viola da gamba and continually repeated, giving the movement as a whole the character of a passacaglia) reflects the words "falsche Zungen stechen." On the other hand, sustained notes and figures are used to depict "patient endurance" ("Geduld"). Hidden in the bass line, and not easily heard, are the notes to the chorale "O Sacred Head Now Wounded."

35. (41.) Tenor Aria

Geduld,	Patience,
wenn mich falsche Zungen stechen.	when false tongues sting me;
Leid ich wider meine Schuld	if, guiltless, I suffer
Schimpf und Spott,	insult and scorn,
ei, so mag der liebe Gott	ah, then may the dear God
meines Herzens Unschuld rächen.	avenge my heart's innocence.

As Jesus faces the High Priest, he is confronted by the question that will ultimately prove to be his undoing: "Are you the Christ?" When Jesus answers affirmatively, he is accused of blasphemy. In the polyphonic texture that follows we hear the priests in growing numbers denounce him as worthy of death.

36a, b, c. (42.) Recitative (Evangelist, High Priest, Jesus) and Chorus

Und der Hohepriester antwortete und sprach zu ihm: Ich beschwöre dich bei dem lebendigen Gott, daß du uns sagest, ob du seiest Christus, der Sohn Gottes? Jesus sprach zu ihm: Du sagests. Doch sage ich euch: Von nun an wirds geschehen, daß ihr sehen werdet des Menschen Sohn sitzen zur Rechten der Kraft und kommen in den Wolken des Himmels. Da zerriß der Hohepriester seine Kleider und sprach: Er hat Gott gelästert, was dürfen wir weiter Zeugnis? Siehe, itzt habt ihr seine Gotteslästerung gehöret. Was dünket euch? Sie antworteten und sprachen: Er ist des Todes schuldig!

And the high priest answered and said to him, "I adjure you by the living God that you tell us whether you are the Christ, the Son of God." Jesus said to him, "You are saying it. But I say to you, from now on you will see the Son of Man sitting at the right hand of power, and come in the clouds of heaven." Then the high priest tore his clothes and said, "He has blasphemed, what need we further witness? See, now you have heard his blasphemy. What do you think?" They answered and said, "He is guilty of death!"

Circling around him, his captors first mock, then brutalize Jesus.

36c, d. (43.) Recitative (Evangelist) and Chorus

Da speieten sie aus in sein Angesicht und schlugen ihn mit Fäusten. Etliche aber schlugen ihn ins Angesicht und sprachen: Weissage uns, Christe, wer ists, der dich schlug?

Then they spat in his face and hit him with fists. A few, however, hit him in the face and said, "Prophesy, Christ, who was it that hit you?"

The congregation responds immediately with disbelief and sorrow. The joint between the two movements is seamless, the hymn beginning with the same chord (F major) that ended the preceding chorus.

37. (44.) Chorale

**Wer hat dich so geschlagen,
mein Heil, und dich mit Plagen
so übel zugericht'?
Du bist ja nicht ein Sünder
wie wir und unsre Kinder;
von Missetaten weißt du nicht.**

Who struck you in this way,
my Salvation; and with torment
treated you so badly?
For you are no sinner
like us and our children;
you know nothing of evildoing.

Now Peter comes to his time of testing. As Jesus had predicted, Peter denies him.

38a, b. (45.) Recitative (Evangelist, First Maid, Second Maid, Peter)

Petrus aber saß draußen im Palast; und es trat zu ihm eine Magd und sprach: Und du warest auch mit dem Jesu aus

But Peter sat outside in the palace, and a maid approached him and said: "And you were also with that Jesus of Galilee."

Galiläa. Er leugnete aber vor ihnen allen und sprach: Ich weiß nicht, was du sagest. Als er aber zur Tür hinausging, sahe ihn eine andere und sprach zu denen, die da waren: Dieser war auch mit dem Jesu von Nazareth. Und er leugnete abermal und schwur dazu: Ich kenne des Menschen nicht. Und über eine kleine Weile traten hinzu, die da stunden, und sprachen zu Petro: Wahrlich, du bist auch einer von denen; denn deine Sprache verrät dich.

But he denied it before them all and said, "I do not know what you are saying." But as he was going out the door another maid saw him and said to those who were there, "This one was also with that Jesus of Nazareth." And he denied it again and swore, "I do not know the man." And after a little while those who were standing there approached and said to Peter, "Truly, you are also one of them, for your speech betrays you."

Becoming ever more vehement, Peter finally swears his denial. Bach highlights this last false statement with a "harmonic mistake": parallel fifths between the vocal line (see the G♯ appoggiatura) and the instrumental bass. Abandoning dispassionate narration, the Evangelist describes Peter's subsequent tears of remorse in a musical passage of unforgettable pathos.

38c. (46.) Recitative (Evangelist and Peter)

Da hub er an, sich zu verfluchen und zu schwören: Ich kenne des Menschen nicht. Und alsbald krähete der Hahn. Da dachte Petrus an die Worte Jesu, da er zu ihm sagte: Ehe der Hahn krähen wird, wirst du mich dreimal verleugnen. Und er ging heraus und weinete bitterlich.

Then he began to call curses down on himself and to swear, "I do not know the man." And immediately the cock crowed. Then Peter remembered the words of Jesus, when he had said to him, "Before the cock crows you will deny me three times. And he went out, and wept bitterly.

Peter's remorse and the descending figure used to depict his weeping serves as the basis for the following alto aria, a movement of profound sadness and a major meditative stopping point in the Passion. The words "erbarme dich mein Gott" remind us of the chorale in the very opening movement ("O Lamm Gottes . . . erbarm dich unser"). However, while the plea for mercy was ecclesiastically objective there, it is now personal and subjective. A further level of commentary is provided by the instrumental bass, into whose line is embedded the opening phrase of the "Passion Chorale."

39. (47.) Alto Aria

Erbarme dich, mein Gott,
um meiner Zähren willen!
Schaue hier,
Herz und Auge weint vor dir bitterlich.
Erbarme dich, mein Gott,
um meiner Zähren willen.

Have mercy, my God,
for my tears' sake!
Look here,
heart and eye weep bitterly before you.
Have mercy, my God,
for my tears' sake.

Identifying with Peter's failure, the choruses (representing the listening congregation) now join in a hymn of corporate confession.

40. (48.) Chorale

Bin ich gleich von dir gewichen,
stell ich mich doch wieder ein;
hat uns doch dein Sohn verglichen
durch sein Angst und Todespein.
Ich verleugne nicht die Schuld;
aber deine Gnad und Huld
ist viel größer als die Sünde,
die ich stets in mir befinde.

Although I have strayed from you,
I now return.
For indeed your Son has reconciled us
through his anguish and pain of death.
I do not deny the guilt,
but your grace and kindness,
is far greater than the sin
which I ever find in me.

With Peter's denial scene concluded we come now to Judas's change of heart. Seeing Jesus handed over to the Roman authorities, he realizes that his teacher will be executed. In two recitatives comprising a total of thirty measures, we hear him return the thirty pieces of silver to the priests.

41a, b. (49.) Recitative (Evangelist and Judas) and Chorus

Des Morgens aber hielten alle Hohen-
priester und die Ältesten des Volks einen
Rat über Jesum, daß sie ihn töteten. Und
bunden ihn, führeten ihn hin und über-
antworteten ihn dem Landpfleger Pontio
Pilato. Da das sahe Judas, der ihn verra-
ten hatte, daß er verdammt war zum
Tode, gereuete es ihn, und brachte her-
wieder die dreißig Silberlinge den
Hohenpriestern und Ältesten und sprach:
Ich habe übel getan, daß ich unschuldig
Blut verraten habe. Sie sprachen: Was
gehet uns das an? Da siehe du zu!

In the morning, however, all the high priests and elders of the people held council concerning Jesus, to put him to death. And they bound him, led him away, and handed him over to the governor, Pontius Pilate. When Judas, who had betrayed him, saw that he was condemned to death, he was remorseful, and he returned the thirty pieces of silver to the high priests and elders, saying, "I have done evil, for I have betrayed innocent blood." They said, "What is that to us? That is your concern."

While Judas commits suicide in despair, the two high priests consider appropriate ways of handling the "blood money." They come to agreement on one point: it would be inappropriate to put the money in the temple treasury. Bach underscores the consensus with synchronized rhythms and parallel sixths.

41c. (50.) Recitative (Evangelist, First Priest, Second Priest)

Und er warf die Silberlinge in den Tem-
pel, hub sich davon, ging hin, und er-
hängete sich selbst. Aber die Hohen-
priester nahmen die Silberlinge und

And he cast the silver pieces into the temple, and turned away, went forth, and hanged himself. But the high priests took the silver pieces and said, "It is not

sprachen: Es taugt nicht, daß wir sie in den Gotteskasten legen, denn es ist Blutgeld.	proper for us to put them in the treasury, for they are blood money."

In the following concerto-like aria, the bass solist protests these events while the strings play emphatic, syncopated "throwing" figures, and a solo violin flings out wild configurations symbolizing the sound of the silver pieces scattering across the temple floor.[10]

42. (51.) Bass Aria

Gebt mir meinen Jesum wieder!	Give me back my Jesus!
Seht, das Geld,	Look, the money,
den Mörderlohn,	the murderer's payment,
wirft euch der verlorne Sohn	that lost son flings
zu den Füßen nieder!	at your feet!
Gebt mir meinen Jesum wieder!	Give me back my Jesus!

After further consultation the religious leaders come to a decision about the money. In an attempt to show how all these events were divinely foreordained, the Evangelist quotes a passage from the book of Jeremiah. Perhaps to show the downward spiral of events the music modulates from E minor to D minor to C minor. Then, to maintain dramatic momentum the story moves on directly to the governor's interrogation of Jesus.

43. (52.) Recitative (Evangelist, Pilate, Jesus)

Sie hielten aber einen Rat und kauften einen Töpfersakker darum zum Begräbnis der Pilger. Daher ist derselbige Acker genennet der Blutakker bis auf den heutigen Tag. Da ist erfüllet, das gesagt ist durch den Propheten Jeremias, da er spricht: "Sie haben genommen dreißig Silberlinge, damit bezahlet ward der Verkaufte, welchen sie kauften von den Kindern Israel, und haben sie gegeben um einen Töpfersakker, als mir der Herr befohlen hat."	But they took counsel among themselves, and bought a potter's field, for the burial of pilgrims. For that reason the field has been known as "the Field of Blood" to this day. Thus was fulfilled what is said by the prophet Jeremiah, who says, "They have taken thirty silver pieces, the price of the one who was sold, whom they bought from the children of Israel, and have given them for a potter's field, as the Lord instructed me."
Jesus aber stund vor dem Landpfleger; und der Landpfleger fragte ihn und sprach: Bist du der Juden König? Jesus aber sprach zu ihm: Du sagsts. Und da er verklagt war von den Hohenpriestern und Ältesten, antwortete er nichts. Da sprach Pilatus zu ihm: Hörest du nicht, wie hart sie dich verklagen? Und er antwortete ihm nicht auf ein Wort, also, daß sich auch der Landpfleger sehr verwunderte.	But Jesus stood before the governor, and the governor asked him, "Are you the king of the Jews?" Jesus said to him, "You are saying it." And when the high priests and elders accused him, he answered nothing. Then Pilate said to him, "Do you not hear how hard they are accusing you?" And he answered not a word, so that even the governor marveled greatly.

The choirs (responding for the congregation) now sing their determination to maintain faith in face of these events. The tune is familiar; it is the "Passion Chorale," appearing for the third time.

44. (53.) Chorale

Befiehl du deine Wege
Und was dein Herze kränkt
der allertreusten Pflege
des, der den Himmel lenkt.
Der Wolken, Luft und Winden
gibt Wege, Lauf und Bahn,
der wird auch Wege finden,
da dein Fuß gehen kann.

Entrust your ways
and whatever grieves your heart
to the ever faithful care
of him who guides the heavens.
He who gives the clouds, air, and winds
their paths, course, and track,
will also find ways
on which your feet may walk.

Though Pilate hopes to release Jesus, the crowd unexpectedly cries for Barabbas instead. The chord Bach uses at this point (a D♯ diminished seventh chord) is not only harmonically unexpected but also (for the time period) harshly dissonant. When Pilate asks what shall be done with Jesus, the agitated mob calls for his crucifixion in jagged melodic lines that incorporate many sharped notes, cross figures, and dissonant intervals.

45a, b. (54.) Recitative (Evangelist, Pilate, Pilate's Wife) and **Chorus**

Auf das Fest aber hatte der Landpfleger Gewohnheit, dem Volk einen Gefangenen loszugeben, welchen sie wollten. Er hatte aber zu der Zeit einen Gefangenen, einen sonderlichen vor andern, der hieß Barrabas. Und da sie versammlet waren, sprach Pilatus zu ihnen: Welchen wollet ihr, daß ich euch losgebe? Barrabam oder Jesum, von dem gesaget wird, er sei Christus? Denn er wußte wohl, daß sie ihn aus Neid überantwortet hatten.

Und da er auf dem Richtstuhl saß, schikkete sein Weib zu ihm und ließ ihm sagen: Habe du nichts zu schaffen mit diesem Gerechten; ich habe heute viel erlitten im Traum von seinetwegen!

Aber die Hohenpriester und die Ältesten überredeten das Volk, daß sie um Barrabas bitten sollten, und Jesum umbrächten. Da antwortete nun der Landpfleger und sprach zu ihnen: Welchen wollt ihr unter diesen zweien, den ich euch soll losgeben? Sie sprachen:

Now the governor had the custom of releasing a prisoner during the festival, whomever the people might choose. At that time he had a notable prisoner named Barabbas. And when they had gathered, Pilate said to them, "Whom do you want for me to release to you: Barabbas or Jesus, of whom it is said he is the Christ?" For he knew full well that they had delivered him up out of envy.

And as he sat in the judgment seat, his wife sent word to him, saying, "Have nothing to do with this man; I have suffered much this day in a dream because of him."

But the high priests and the elders persuaded the people to ask for Barabbas and to have Jesus killed. Then the governor answered and said to them, "Which of these two do you want me to release to you?" They said, "Barabbas!"

Barrabam! Pilatus sprach zu ihnen: Was soll ich denn machen mit Jesu, von dem gesagt wird, er sei Christus? Sie sprachen alle: Laß ihn kreuzigen!

Pilate said to them, "What shall I then do with Jesus, who is said to be Christ?" They all said, "Let him be crucified!"

Removing themselves somewhat from the immediate scene, the choirs ponder the theological significance of this perversion of justice in language that recalls the earlier theme of the Good Shepherd.

46. (55.) Chorale

Wie wunderbarlich
ist doch diese Strafe!
Der gute Hirte
leidet für die Schafe,
die Schuld bezahlt
der Herre, der Gerechte,
für seine Knechte.

How wonderfully strange
is this punishment!
The good shepherd
suffers for the sheep;
The lord, the righteous one,
pays the debt
for his servants.

47. (56.) Recitative (Evangelist and Pilate)
Der Landpfleger sagte: Was hat er denn Übels getan?

The governor said, "What wrong has he done then?"

When Pilate asks what crime Jesus has committed, the soprano answers even before the Evangelist can respond, recounting his many good deeds. The mood, reinforced by the accompanying oboes da caccia, is one of pastoral tranquility.

48. (57.) Soprano Recitative
Er hat uns allen wohlgetan,
den Blinden gab er das Gesicht,
die Lahmen macht' er gehend,
er sagt' uns seines Vaters Wort,
er trieb die Teufel fort,
Betrübte hat er aufgericht',
er nahm die Sünder auf und an.
Sonst hat mein Jesus nichts getan.

He has done good to us all;
the blind he gave their sight,
the lame he made to walk,
he proclaimed his Father's word to us,
he drove out demons,
the dejected he raised up,
he received and accepted sinners;
otherwise my Jesus has done nothing.

The soprano aria that follows is the architectural centerpiece of the entire work. Two striking musical features are the absence of a continuo bass and the frequent intrusion of fermatas (i.e., pauses). It is as if the soloist is benumbed in a private, disembodied state of shock and disbelief. The presence of the flute and oboes da caccia provide a pastoral ambience; now however, Jesus is no longer pictured as a shepherd but as an innocent lamb.

49. (58.) Soprano Aria

Aus Liebe will mein Heiland sterben,	Out of love my Lord is dying,
von einer Sünde, weiß er nichts,	of sin he knows nothing,
daß das ewige Verderben	so that eternal perdition
und die Strafe des Gerichts	and the punishment of judgment
nicht auf meiner Seele bliebe.	should not remain upon my soul.

Again the crowd calls for crucifixion. The music is the same as before but transposed up one tone, intensifying the effect. When Pilate sees he is getting nowhere, he yields to the mob.

50a, b, c, d, e. (59.) Recitative (Evangelist and Pilate) and **Chorus**

Sie schrieen aber noch mehr, und sprachen: Laß ihn kreuzigen! Da aber Pilatus sahe, daß er nichts schaffete, sondern daß ein viel größer Getümmel ward, nahm er Wasser und wusch die Hände vor dem Volk und sprach: Ich bin unschuldig an dem Blut dieses Gerechten, sehet ihr zu. Da antwortete das ganze Volk und sprach: Sein Blut komme über uns und unsre Kinder. Da gab er ihnen Barrabam los: aber Jesus ließ er geißeln und überantwortete ihn, daß er gekreuziget würde.	But they cried out even more and said, "Let him be crucified!" Now when Pilate saw that he was accomplishing nothing, but rather that the tumult was getting much greater, he took water and washed his hands before the people and said, "I am innocent of the blood of this righteous person; you see to it." Then all the people answered and said, "His blood be on us and on our children." Then he released Barabbas to them; but he had Jesus scourged, and delivered him over to be crucified.

While the strings of the orchestra depict the scourging of Jesus, the alto soloist, greatly agitated, pleads for mercy.

51. (60.) Alto Recitative

Erbarm es Gott!	May God have mercy!
Hier steht der Heiland angebunden.	Here the Savior stands, bound.
O Geißelung, o Schläg, o Wunden!	O scourging, O blows, O wounds!
Ihr Henker, haltet ein!	You tormentors, stop!
Erweichet euch der Seelen Schmerz,	Does the sight of such agony of soul,
der Anblick solches Jammers nicht?	such misery, not soften you?
Ach ja! ihr habt ein Herz,	Ah yes, you have a heart;
das muß der Martersäule gleich	it must be like a whipping post,
und noch viel härter sein.	but even much harder.
Erbarmt euch, haltet ein!	Have pity, stop!

Desperate yet helpless to provide aid, the alto expresses her great sadness in an emotionally charged aria. The scourging figure of the previous movement continues here in a slower rhythm, while wavelike figures suggest the flowing of tears and blood. The aria's considerable length serves the important dramatic function of providing a pause between the trial scene and the crucifixion scene.

52. (61.) Alto Aria

Können Tränen meiner Wangen nichts erlangen,	If the tears on my cheeks can achieve nothing,
o, so nehmt mein Herz hinein!	oh, then take my heart!
Aber laßt es bei den Fluten,	But for the streams that flow
wenn die Wunden milde bluten,	when your wounds bleed tenderly,
auch die Opferschale sein!	let it also be the altar chalice!

In the crucifixion scene the choruses play the part of the Roman soldiers, who mock and taunt Jesus from all sides.

53a, b. (62.) Recitative (Evangelist) and Chorus

Da nahmen die Kriegsknechte des Land-pflegers Jesum zu sich in das Richthaus und sammleten über ihn die ganze Schar und zogen ihn aus, und legeten ihm einen Purpurmantel an und flochten eine dornene Krone und satzten sie auf sein Haupt und ein Rohr in seine rechte Hand und beugeten die Knie vor ihm, und spotteten ihn und sprachen: Gegrüßet seist du, Jüdenkönig! Und speieten ihn an und nahmen das Rohr und schlugen damit sein Haupt.

Then the governor's soldiers took Jesus with them into the judgment hall and gathered the entire cohort around him, stripped off his clothes and put a purple robe on him, and wove a crown of thorns and put it on his head, and a reed in his right hand, and bowed the knee before him and mocked him, saying, "Hail, King of the Jews!" And spat on him, and took the reed, and struck his head with it.

The blows to Jesus' head provides the immediate thematic connection to the hymn that follows. Torn between reverent awe and distress for the suffering Christ, the choirs meditate on the mistreatment of Jesus with familiar stanzas of the "Passion Chorale." The hymn tune appears here for the fourth time, and in its highest key. Perhaps Bach meant to draw attention to these two stanzas (with their emphasis on Jesus' wounds); certainly Bach's fivefold use of the tune throughout the course of the work suggests the possibility of a symbolic reference to the five stigmata.

54. (63.) Chorale

O Haupt voll Blut und Wunden,	O head covered with blood and wounds,
voll Schmerz und voller Hohn,	heaped with pain and scorn,
o Haupt, zu Spott gebunden,	O head, for mocking bound
mit einer Dornenkron,	with a crown of thorns,
o Haupt, sonst schön gezieret	O head, once beautifully adorned,
mit höchster Ehr und Zier,	with highest honor and decoration
jetzt aber hoch schimpfieret,	but now highly reviled,
gegrüßet seist du mir!	Let me greet you!

Du edles Angesichte,	O countenance so noble,
dafür sonst schrickt und scheut	before which the whole world
das große Weltgewichte,	otherwise shrinks in fear and awe,
wie bist du so bespeit;	how you are spat upon;
wie bist du so erbleichet!	how pale you have grown!
Wer hat dein Augenlicht,	Who mistreated
dem sonst kein Licht	the light of your eyes,
nicht gleichet,	which no other light can equal,
so schändlich zugericht'?	so shamefully?

55. (64.) Recitative (Evangelist)

Und da sie ihn verspottet hatten, zogen sie ihm den Mantel aus und zogen ihm seine Kleider an und führeten ihn hin, daß sie ihn kreuzigten. Und indem sie hinausgingen, funden sie einen Menschen von Kyrene mit Namen Simon; den zwungen sie, daß er ihm sein Kreuz trug.

And after they had mocked him, they took the robe off him, and dressed him in his own clothes, and led him to be crucified. And as they were going out they found a man from Cyrene by the name of Simon; him they compelled to carry his cross for him.

In the following reflective recitative the bass soloist generalizes the previous text in a meditation on the theological significance of cross-bearing. The inherent bittersweet nature of cross-bearing is reflected in Bach's instrumentation and harmonic materials: a viola da gamba plays chromatically variegated arpeggios, which are echoed by two flutes, outlined melodically in parallel thirds and sixths. The recitative is marked "a battuta," indicating that it is to be performed in strict rhythm. The result is a measured rhythm that adds a sense of resignation.

56. (65.) Bass Recitative

Ja freilich will in uns	Yea, truly must
das Fleisch und Blut	our flesh and blood
zum Kreuz gezwungen sein;	be compelled to bear the cross;
je mehr es unsrer Seele gut,	the better it is for our soul,
je herber geht es ein.	the more bitter it is to bear.

The theme of personal cross-bearing reappears in the aria, which, after the arias "Erbarme dich" and "Aus Liebe," is the "third major stopping point on the way of Christ to the cross. . . . The speaker . . . wishes to relieve Jesus of the cross, though requesting the aid of Jesus for his own burden, understood at a second level as the cross of one's personal fate."[11] As in the tenor aria "Geduld," Bach embeds the notes of the opening phrase of "O Sacred Head Now Wounded" in the instrumental bass line, which like No. 35 (41) features the viola da gamba in a halting, jabbing rhythm.

57. (66.) Bass Aria

Komm, süßes Kreuz, so will ich sagen,	Come, sweet cross, so will I say,
mein Jesu, gib es immer her!	my Jesus, give it ever to me!
Wird mir mein Leiden einst zu schwer,	If my suffering ever becomes too great,
so hilfst du mir es selber tragen.	you yourself will help me bear it.

A long yet relatively straightforward recitative describes the crucifixion itself. Sharps (= *Kreuze*) appear everywhere in the music. Passersby mockingly repeat one of Jesus' statements that (along with others) had been interpreted by his accusers as a claim to divinity and so led to his ultimate undoing. The religious leaders similarly mock him with his own record. As if to suggest that all standing there are unanimous about the nature of the issue in question, Bach has the chorus end with a forceful unison passage—the only one in the entire Passion—on the words "He said, 'I am God's Son.'"

58a. (67.) Recitative (Evangelist) and
Chorus

Und da sie an die Stätte kamen mit Namen Golgatha, das ist verdeutschet Schädelstätt, gaben sie ihm Essig zu trinken mit Gallen vermischet; und da ers schmekkete, wollte ers nicht trinken. Da sie ihn aber gekreuziget hatten, teilten sie seine Kleider und wurfen das Los darum, auf daß erfüllet würde, das gesagt ist durch den Propheten: "Sie haben meine Kleider unter sich geteilet, und über mein Gewand haben sie das Los geworfen."
Und sie saßen allda, und hüteten sein. Und oben zu seinen Häupten hefteten sie die Ursach seines Todes beschrieben, nämlich: "Dies ist Jesus, der Juden König." Und da wurden zween Mörder mit ihm gekreuziget, einer zur Rechten und einer zur Linken. Die aber vorübergingen, lästerten ihn und schüttelten ihre Köpfe und sprachen: Der du den Tempel Gottes zerbrichst und bauest ihn in dreien Tagen, hilf dir selber! Bist du Gottes Sohn, so steig herab vom Kreuz!
Desgleichen auch die Hohenpriester spotteten sein samt den Schriftgelehrten und Ältesten und sprachen: Andern hat er geholfen und kann ihm selber nicht helfen. Ist er der König Israel, so steige er nun vom Kreuz, so wollen wir ihm

And when they came to the place called Golgotha (which may be translated, "Place of the Skull") they gave him vinegar to drink mixed with gall; and when he tasted it he did not want to drink it. Now when they had crucified him they divided his garments and cast lots for them, so that what is said by the prophets might be fulfilled: "They have divided my garments among them, and for my raiment they have cast lots."

And they sat down there and kept watch over him. And above his head they fastened the reason for his death, namely, "This is Jesus, the King of the Jews! And two murderers were crucified with him, one to the right and one to the left. But those who passed by reviled him and wagged their heads, saying, "You who destroy the temple of God and build it in three days, help yourself! If you are God's son, then step down from the cross!"

In the same way the high priests also mocked him, with the scribes and elders, saying, "He helped others and cannot help himself. If he is the king of Israel, let him step down from the cross; then we will believe him. He trusted in God; let

glauben. *Er hat Gott vertrauet, der erlöse* him deliver him now if he will, for he said,
ihn nun, lüstets ihn; denn er hat gesagt: "I am God's son."
Ich bin Gottes Sohn.

58b. (68.) Recitative (Evangelist)
Desgleichen schmäheten ihn auch die   In the same way the murderers, who
Mörder, die mit ihm gekreuziget waren.   were crucified with him, also reviled him.

In an intimate tone the alto soloist sings her sorrow, while pondering the paradox inherent in the crucifixion: to save others he could not save himself. The unique instrumentation (two oboes da caccia, pizzicato cello, and bass) and a repetitive motivic construction produce a mood of quiet resignation.

59. (69.) Alto Recitative
Ach Golgatha, unselges Golgatha!   Ah Golgotha, accursed Golgotha!
Der Herr der Herrlichkeit muß   the Lord of Glory must
schimpflich hier verderben,   perish here in disgrace;
der Segen und das Heil der Welt   the Blessing and Salvation of the world
wird als ein Fluch ans Kreuz gestellt.   is put on the cross like a curse.
Der Schöpfer Himmels und der Erden   The creator of heaven and earth
soll Erd und Luft entzogen werden.   is deprived of earth and air.
Die Unschuld muß hier   Innocence must here
schuldig sterben,   die guilty;
das gehet meiner Seele nah;   this cuts me to the quick.
Ach Golgatha, unselges Golgatha!   Ah Golgotha, accursed Golgotha!

As usual, reflection continues in an aria—here a tender, comforting movement, in whose dialogue (between soloist and chorus) onlookers are encouraged to find solace and redemption in the outstretched arms of the crucified one. The text alludes to Jesus' lament in Matthew 23:37 that he had often wanted to gather the "children of Jerusalem" like a hen gathers her chicks under her wings, but they had been unwilling, an allusion also found in Cantata 40. Two oboes da caccia, continuously repeating circular motives in parallel thirds and sixths against a walking arpeggiated bass line (which is marked "pizzicato" for the cellos), play the role of the little chicks.

60. (70.) Alto Aria and **Chorus**
Sehet, Jesus hat die Hand,   Look, Jesus has stretched out
uns zu fassen, ausgespannt,   his hand to clasp us,
kommt!   Come!
  Wohin?   Where?
    . . . in Jesu Armen,   . . . into Jesus' arms
sucht Erlösung, nehmt Erbarmen.   seek redemption, receive mercy.
Suchet!   Seek!
  Wo?   Where?

... in Jesu Armen.	... in Jesus' arms.
Lebet, sterbet, ruhet hier,	Live, die, rest here,
ihr verlaßnen Küchlein ihr.	you forsaken little chicks,
Bleibet ...	stay ...
Wo?	Where?
... in Jesu Armen.	... in Jesus' arms.

As the moment of death approaches, Jesus cries out—a desperate prayer asking why God has forsaken him. Here the "halo of strings" that usually accompanies his speech is conspicuously and symbolically absent. Since the cry (seemingly a quotation from Psalm 22) is first rendered in the original Aramaic, then in translation, Bach has the opportunity to present it twice: first in a lower range by Jesus, then in a higher, intensified one by the Evangelist. Meanwhile, some bystanders, more interested in eschatology than in another's suffering, conjecture that he is calling Elijah, whose return had been foretold.

61a, b, c, d. (71.) Recitative (Evangelist and Jesus) and Chorus

Und von der sechsten Stunde an war eine Finsternis über das ganze Land bis zu der neunten Stunde. Und um die neunte Stunde schrie Jesus laut und sprach: Eli, Eli, lama, lama, asabthani? Das ist: Mein Gott, mein Gott, warum hast du mich verlassen?	And from the sixth hour onward darkness came over the entire land, until the ninth hour. And at the ninth hour Jesus cried loudly, and said, "Eli, Eli, lama, lama, sabachthani!" That is, "My God, my God, why then have you forsaken me?"
Etliche aber, die da stunden, da sie das höreten, sprachen sie: Der rufet dem Elias! Und bald lief einer unter ihnen, nahm einen Schwamm und füllete ihn mit Essig und stekkte ihn auf ein Rohr und tränkete ihn. Die andern aber sprachen: Halt! laß sehen, ob Elias komme und ihm helfe? Aber Jesus schriee abermal laut, und verschied.	But when some of those standing there heard it, they said, "He is calling Elijah!" And immediately one of them ran, took a sponge and filled it with vinegar, and fastened it upon a reed, and gave him to drink. But the others said, "Wait! Let us see whether Elijah will come and help him." But Jesus cried loudly a second time, and expired.

Considering Jesus' dying cry, the chorus now sings the "Passion Chorale" tune for the fifth and final time, praying not to be forsaken by the crucified one in the hour of death. Bach's harmonization is more chromatic this time, increasing the hymn's subjective focus and expressive effectiveness.

62. (72.) Chorale

Wenn ich einmal soll scheiden,	When I one day shall depart,
so scheide nicht von mir,	then part not from me.
wenn ich den Tod soll leiden,	When I must suffer death,
so tritt du denn herfür!	then come to my side.
Wenn mir am allerbängsten	When I am most afraid
wird um das Herze sein,	in my heart,

so reiß mich aus den Ängsten	then save me from those fears
kraft deiner Angst und Pein!	by virtue of your fear and pain.

Supernatural events follow Jesus' death. The tearing of the temple curtain and the earthquake are vividly depicted in the continuo bass. In his excitement, the Evangelist swoops to a high B♭ three times. As the centurion and soldiers observe the supernatural phenomena, faith begins to dawn, and they confess their realization in an awestruck creedal statement. Without pause we are told next of the women who were also there, and Joseph, who asks for Jesus' body.

63a, b. (73.) Recitative (Evangelist) and Chorus

Und siehe da, der Vorhang im Tempel zerriß in zwei Stück von obenan bis untenaus. Und die Erde erbebete, und die Felsen zerrissen, und die Gräber täten sich auf, und stunden auf viel Leiber der Heiligen, die da schliefen, und gingen aus den Gräbern nach seiner Auferstehung und kamen in die heilige Stadt und erschienen vielen. Aber der Hauptmann und die bei ihm waren und bewahreten Jesum, da sie sahen das Erdbeben und was da geschah, erschraken sie sehr und sprachen: Wahrlich, dieser ist Gottes Sohn gewesen.	And behold, the veil of the temple tore in two pieces, from top to bottom. And the earth shook, and the rocks were split, and the graves opened, and there rose up many bodies of the saints who were sleeping, who went out of their graves after his resurrection and came into the holy city, appearing to many. But when the captain and those who were with him keeping watch over Jesus saw the earthquake and the things that happened, they were terrified and said, "Truly this was the Son of God."
Und es waren viel Weiber da, die von ferne zusahen, die da waren nachgefolget aus Galiäa, und hatten ihm gedienet, unter welchen war Maria Magdalena, und Maria, die Mutter Jacobi und Joses, und die Mutter der Kinder Zebedäi.	And many women were there, watching from afar, who had followed him from Galilee, and had ministered to him, among whom was Mary Magdalene and Mary, the mother of James and of Joseph, and the mother of Zebedee's children.
Am Abend aber kam ein reicher Mann von Arimathia, der hieß Joseph, welcher auch ein Jünger Jesu war, der ging zu Pilato, und bat ihn um den Leichnam Jesu. Da befahl Pilatus, man sollte ihm ihn geben.	But in the evening, there came a wealthy man from Arimathea, by the name of Joseph, who was also one of Jesus' disciples; he went to Pilate and asked for the body of Jesus. Then Pilate ordered that it be given to him.

Following the narrator's reference to the events of that evening, the bass soloist contemplates evening as a time of conclusion, reviewing other nocturnal biblical stories of closure, and the significance of receiving Jesus' body in the Eucharist. "Peace" and "rest" are symbolized by held notes in the instrumental bass, while restlessness is expressed in the trembling of the violins and in the harmony, which changes continually.

64. (74.) Bass Recitative

Am Abend, da es kühle war,	In the evening, when it was cool,
ward Adams Fallen offenbar;	Adam's fall was made manifest;
am Abend	in the evening
drükket ihn der Heiland nieder.	the Savior overwhelmed it.
Am Abend kam die Taube wieder	In the evening the dove returned
und trug ein Ölblatt in dem Munde.	with an olive leaf in her bill.
O schöne Zeit! O Abendstunde!	O lovely time! O evening hour!
Der Friedensschluß	Peace with God
ist nun mit Gott gemacht,	has now been made,
denn Jesus hat sein Kreuz vollbracht.	for Jesus has accomplished his cross.
Sein Leichnam kömmt zur Ruh,	His body comes to rest;
ach! liebe Seele, bitte du,	ah, dear soul, ask,
geh,	go,
lasse dir den toten Jesum schenken,	let them give you the dead Jesus,
o heilsames,	O salutary,
o köstlichs Angedenken!	O precious remembrance!

Set in the relative major key of the foregoing movement, and employing the lilting rhythm of the siciliano (a pastoral dance), the bass aria continues with the literary idea of rest, joyfully describing the peace and certainty of salvation through mystic union with Jesus.

65. (75.) Bass Aria

Mache dich, mein Herze, rein,	My heart, purify yourself;
ich will Jesum selbst begraben.	I want to bury Jesus myself.
Denn er soll nunmehr in mir	For henceforth he shall find in me
für und für	for ever and ever,
seine süße Ruhe haben.	his sweet rest.
Welt, geh aus, laß Jesum ein!	World, begone, let Jesus in!

After Jesus is buried, the religious leaders come en masse to Pilate. For their utterance Bach employs all forces: both choirs and both orchestras. The resulting aggressiveness contrasts sharply with the meditative tone of the surrounding movements. When the leaders tell of Jesus' promise to rise from the dead after three days, their lines rise imitatively, beginning from lowest voices to highest.

66a. (76.) Recitative (Evangelist) and
Chorus

Und Joseph nahm den Leib und wikkelte ihn in ein rein Leinwand und legte ihn in sein eigen neu Grab, welches er hatte lassen in einen Fels hauen, und wälzete einen großen Stein vor die Tür des Grabes, und ging davon. Es war aber allda Maria Magdalena und die andere Maria, die satzten sich gegen das Grab. Des andern Tages, der da folget nach dem	And Joseph took the body and wrapped it in a clean linen cloth and laid it in his own new tomb, which he had hewn out of the rock, and rolled a large stone in front of the door of the tomb, and went away. But Mary Magdalene and the other Mary were there; they seated themselves opposite the grave. The next day (the one following the day of preparation) the

Rüsttage, kamen die Hohenpriester und
Pharisäer sämtlich zu Pilato, und sprachen: Herr, wir haben gedacht, daß dieser Verführer sprach, da er noch lebete:
Ich will nach dreien Tagen wieder auf-
erstehen. Darum befiehl, daß man das
Grab verwahre bis an den dritten Tag,
auf daß nicht seine Jünger kommen und
stehlen ihn und sagen zu dem Volk: Er
ist auferstanden von den Toten, und
werde der letzte Betrug ärger denn der
erste! Pilatus sprach zu ihnen: Da habt
ihr die Hüter; gehet hin und verwahrets,
wie ihrs wisset! Sie gingen hin und ver-
wahreten das Grab mit Hütern, und
versiegelten den Stein.

high priests and Pharisees together
came to Pilate and said, "Sir, we remember that while he was still living this de-
ceiver said, 'I will rise after three days.'
Therefore command that the grave be
secured until the third day, so that his
disciples do not come and steal him and
say to the people, 'He has arisen from
the dead,' and the last deception be
worse than the first!" Pilate said to them,
"There you have watchmen, go and
make it as secure as you know how."
They went forth, and secured the tomb
with watchmen, and sealed the stone.

In a recitative involving both choirs and orchestras, the solo voices of
Chorus I in successive ascending order (B, T, A, S) offer subjective
expressions of contrition and farewell at the grave, while Chorus II
responds with a corporate statement of farewell.

**67. (77.) S. A. T. B. Recitative and Cho-
rus**

Nun ist der Herr zur Ruh gebracht.
    Mein Jesu, gute Nacht!
Die Müh ist aus,
die unsre Sünden ihm gemacht.
    Mein Jesus, gute Nacht!
O selige Gebeine,
seht, wie ich euch
mit Buß und Reu beweine,
daß euch mein Fall
in solche Not gebracht!
    Mein Jesu, gute Nacht!
Habt lebenslang
vor euer Leiden
tausend Dank,
daß ihr mein Seelenheil
so wert geacht'.
    Mein Jesu, gute Nacht!

Now the Lord is laid to rest.
    My Jesus, good night!
The travail,
which our sins made for him, is over.
    My Jesus, good night!
O blessed limbs,
see, how I weep for you
in penitence and remorse,
that my fall
brought you such trouble!
    My Jesus, good night!
May you have, my whole life long,
for your suffering,
a thousandfold thanks,
because you valued my soul's salvation
so highly.
    My Jesus, good night!

The Passion ends with a monumental double chorus in C minor complet-
ing the literary idea of rest and peace. It counterbalances the very opening
movement with its massiveness, and answers that movement's call to
lamentation. The movement is cast in A-B-A form, with a solemn primary
section in which the two orchestras and choirs perform in unison—with
the exception of antiphonal echos on the words "ruhe sanfte – sanfte ruh."
In the contrasting middle section the musical forces are used antiphonally,

and the tonality is less stable. Here listeners are pointed "away from the grave to the meaning of Christ's death. [The] theological and expressive high point is the triple echo of 'Höchstvergnügt schlummern da die Augen ein.'"[12] Thereupon the heavy opening section is repeated.

68. (78.) Chorus

Wir setzen uns mit Tränen nieder	We seat ourselves with tears,
und rufen dir im Grabe zu:	and call to you in the tomb:
Ruhe sanfte, sanfte ruh!	rest gently, gently rest!
Ruht, ihr ausgesognen Glieder!	Rest, you exhausted limbs!
Ruhet sanfte, ruhet wohl!	Rest gently, rest well!
Euer Grab und Leichenstein	Your grave and tombstone
soll dem ängstlichen Gewissen	shall be for the uneasy conscience,
ein bequemes Ruhekissen	a comfortable pillow of rest
und der Seelen Ruhstatt sein.	and a place for the soul to rest.
Höchst vergnügt,	There, in utter delight,
schlummern da die Augen ein.	our eyes shall fall asleep.

Notes

1. Helmuth Rilling, "Helmuth Rilling on *St. Matthew Passion*," CD booklet, Bach, *St. Matthew Passion*, CBS M3K 79403, p. 57.

2. Robin Leaver, "St. Matthew Passion," in Boyd, *Oxford Composer Companions: J. S. Bach*, 432.

3. The first number follows the numbering system used in the new critical edition of Bach's works: *Johann Sebastian Bach: Neue Bach-Ausgabe sämtlicher Werke* (*NBA*), ed. Johann-Sebastian-Bach-Institut Göttingen, and Bach-Archiv Leipzig (Leipzig and Kassel, 1954–). The second number (in parentheses) follows the system used in the *Bach-Werke-Verzeichnis* (BWV); see Wolfgang Schmieder, *Thematisches Verzeichnis der musikalischen Werke von Johann Sebastian Bach*, rev. and expanded ed. (Wiesbaden: Breitkopf and Härtel, 1990).

4. Helmuth Rilling, trans. Kenneth Nafziger, *J. S. Bach - St. Matthew Passion* (New York: C. F. Peters, 1975), 14.

5. Rilling, *St. Matthew Passion*, 14.

6. See Exodus 12:17–20.

7. Rilling, *St. Matthew Passion*, 25.

8. John 13:1.

9. Deuteronomy 19:15.

10. Rilling, *St. Matthew Passion*, 62.

11. Rilling, *St. Matthew Passion*, 71.

12. Rilling, *St. Matthew Passion*, 85–86.

4
Mass in B Minor (BWV 232)

On July 27, 1733, Johann Sebastian Bach sent a set of beautifully prepared parts of a Kyrie and Gloria to the elector of Saxony, Frederick Augustus II (1696–1763), who had succeeded his father, August the Strong, a few months previously. (Two years later, after a successful election to the Polish throne, he would become August III of Poland.) In the letter accompanying the gift, Bach wrote:

> To His Most Serene Highness, the Prince and Lord, Frederick Augustus, Royal Prince in Poland and Lithuania, Duke in Saxony . . .

> To Your Royal Highness I submit in deepest devotion the present small work of that science which I have achieved in musique, with the most wholly submissive prayer that Your Highness will look upon it with Most Gracious Eyes, according to Your Highness's World-Famous Clemency and not according to the poor composition; and thus deign to take me under Your Most Mighty Protection. For some years and up to the present moment, I have had the Directorium of the Music in the two principal churches in Leipzig, but have innocently had to suffer one injury or another, and on occasion also a diminution of the fees accruing to me in this office; but these injuries would disappear altogether if Your Royal Highness would grant me the favor of conferring upon me a title of Your Highness's Court Capelle, and would let Your High Command for the issuing of such a document go forth to the proper place. Such a most gracious fulfillment of my most humble prayer will bind me to unending devotion, and I offer myself in most indebted obedience to show at all times, upon Your Royal Highness's Most

Gracious Desire, my untiring zeal in the composition of music for the
church as well as for the orchestra, and to devote my entire forces to the
service of Your Highness, remaining in unceasing fidelity Your Royal
Highness's most humble and most obedient servant. . . .

Johann Sebastian Bach[1]

With these words the unhappy cantor of St. Thomas introduced the first
part of what is now regarded as an artistic monument of Western civiliza-
tion, his *Mass in B Minor*. While the work that Bach sent to the ruler in
Dresden included only the Kyrie and Gloria portions of the mass ordinary,
Bach would probably have considered it complete for such "short" mass
settings were typical in Lutheran Germany at that time. It was perhaps
Bach's first attempt at setting the Kyrie and Gloria texts—the other four
extant masses were all written later—and it was apparently his most
ambitious: the scope of this *missa* is far beyond that of most *missae brevis*.
Incorporating twelve movements lasting about forty-five minutes, it more
closely approximates the "monumental celebratory settings that were
performed on special occasions in the Dresden *Hofkirche*."[2] Furthermore,
aspects of style and structure reveal that this *missa* has an internal unity
of its own. All five voices are utilized in the solo movements, the instrumental families are represented in turn in the solo instrumental roles, and
various aspects of symmetry can be identified.

The complete mass was not assembled until the very end of Bach's
life. Sometime between August 1748 and October 1749 the various
movements (many of them adaptations from previous works) were
gathered and numbered into three primary divisions: the *missa* became
No. 1, the Credo (*Symbolum Nicenum*) became No. 2; the Sanctus, No. 3;
and the Osanna / Benedictus / Agnus Dei et / Dona nobis pacem, No. 4.[3]
The result was a work of grand proportions. Lasting close to two hours, it
would have been too long for most liturgical settings. Why did Bach write
such an unusually long work? Was it ever performed during Bach's
lifetime? Why were the movements divided into four nonliturgical
sections? Why did an apparently staunchly Lutheran composer write a
Catholic mass in the first place? Did he even conceive of the work as a
unified whole?

Concerning the last question Andreas Bomba writes:

> The unusual diversity of its origins could easily give cause to doubt that
> the *Mass in B Minor* was conceived as a single piece of music. It would
> seem rather that Bach collected individual movements scattered
> throughout his work into a sort of *pasticcio*. Of course, this view is
> based on a notion of creating and composing music which is not

inherent but imposed from without: that a work of art must be "original," composed of fresh ingredients, so to speak, with the conception preceding the composition. A closer look reveals that this premise does not accurately describe what really took place in the course of music history. The mere fact that Bach combined the various portions and composed new music for certain sections as needed proves that a different notion of the creative process is perfectly justifiable: the act of composition need not be restricted to individual notes, the smallest units of music, but can also consist in the creation of an inventive synthesis of larger elements, from quoting motifs and melodies to organizing entire movements and pieces in an artistic arrangement.[4]

Why did Bach compile this great mass? As a universal statement of Christian faith? That is the view of some scholars, including Yoshitake Kobayashi, whose research is responsible for the chronological redesignation of the work, demonstrating that it was Bach's last creative endeavor—his *opus ultimum*.[5] Other scholars suggest that Bach was motivated by a desire for a achieving a supreme artistic expression in a timeless art form. Thus Georg von Dadelsen writes:

As a whole, this Mass has no place in the Lutheran worship service, and at the same time it is unlikely that it was expressly written for a particular catholic rite. . . . Bach probably wished to compose in a field that represented the highest achievement since the time of Josquin and Palestrina, who elevated the Mass to an independent work of art. Bach took it outside the realm of the liturgy, as an expression of his personal mastery.[6]

Christoph Wolff notes the compendium of styles represented by the work and writes:

More traditions attach to the Mass than to any other form of vocal music, and it has indeed been regarded since the fourteenth-century as the central genre of sacred vocal music, so it is not surprising if Bach wanted to write his own contribution to this particular chapter in the history of music.[7]

Similarly, John Butt writes:

Historically the work is an exhaustive—if not didactic— summation of the composer's skills, and of all the styles, idioms and devices available to his age. Bach clearly viewed the mass genre as the most historically durable form. . . . The concepts of hard work, thoroughness and of following an established order to its furthest implications [so character-

istic of Bach], are evident both in the genesis of the *Mass in B Minor*—
obviously aiming towards the perfection and unification of pre-existent
material—and in the sheer density of the resulting work.[8]

Nevertheless, the work has too many marks of intended performance to be
an abstract work for posterity: the extroverted nature of certain movements
(which seem calculated to appeal to an audience of Bach's time), the
structure of the manuscript (loose gatherings typical of Bach's performance scores and four title pages listing the forces needed for each
section), and the revision of the previously existing Sanctus to correspond
to the voicing of the other movements.[9]

Several of the work's features point to Dresden: five-part, SSATB
vocal scoring (unusual for Bach and impractical in Leipzig), extensive
length (similar to that of settings by other Dresden composers), emphasis
on antique polyphonic style, juxtaposition of contrasting styles, emphasis
on chorus writing, and formal division of the work into sections (which
appear in separate folders).[10] Whatever, Bach's motivation, the resulting
work exhibits remarkable unity and dramatic power.

Kyrie

The Kyrie opens with a solemn and grand motto introduction. While such
chordal prefatory statements were unusual for Bach, they were common
in works by Dresden composers. Indeed, it is possible that Bach was
working from a specific model here: a Mass in G Minor by Johann Hugo
von Wilderer, which Bach copied out and apparently also performed
around 1730.[11] Noteworthy is the incorporation of Luther's Kyrie melody
(from the German Mass of 1526) in the uppermost line.[12] Because Bach
used this liturgical melody in other works as well (the Mass in F, BWV
233, and the single Kyrie, BWV 233a)[13] we may assume that its appearance here is significant.

The Kyrie fugue constituting the bulk of the movement is a marvel of
linear tension. The contour of the primary theme (also related to Luther's
traditional cantus firmus[14]) masterfully depicts the text, an anguished plea
for divine mercy. We hear the melody inching slowly and chromatically
upward; several times it falls back abruptly, as if struggling out of a deep
and dark abyss. The tension of this "complex, emotionally charged
subject" is released only in the piccardy-third cadence of the final measure.[15] "A clue to Bach's thinking is provided by his Weimar colleague
Johann Gottfried Walther, who [once] described writing a solemn Kyrie

on the hymn "Aus tiefer Not schrei ich zu dir" ("Out of the depths have I cried unto thee, O Lord"), Luther's paraphrase of Psalm 130."[16] The image is strengthened in the second vocal development where the voices enter sequentially from lowest to highest. The overall sense of anguish is heightened by the appearance of disjointed sighing figures occurring in the middle of text syllables, powerfully portraying the sheer inarticulateness of the speaker.

(Note: For the convenience of readers using music scores employing the older numbering system rather than the one used in the new collected edition, movement numbers are given here according to both schemes whenever they differ.[17])

1. Chorus
Kyrie eleison.   Lord, have mercy.

Of the second movement, George Stauffer writes:

> In the "Christe eleison" Bach moves from the elevated world of the chorus fugue to the intimate realm of the [Neapolitan] love duet . . . [with] dulcet parallel thirds and sixths (emphasized here through sustained notes), diatonic melodic lines, a *galant* mixture of duple and triple figures, straightforward harmonies, expressive appoggiaturas, and weak-beat phrase endings that resolve downward as "sighs."[18]

Set in D major, the relative major (i.e., companion key) of B minor, the key of the previous movement, the "Christe" offers a distinct contrast in tonality, style, and effect. It had long been common practice to make the "Christe" more intimate than the surrounding "Kyrie" statements, often by reducing the choral forces, but Bach achieves even greater contrast by setting the text as a duet in theatrical style. Though not in Da capo form, the movement is unified by means of a ritornello (a harmonically stable, instrumental "refrain"). While duets were often structured as dialogues, this one is different: the voices sing mostly in parallel motion, suggesting agreement between the two singers.

2. Soprano I and Soprano II Duet
Christe eleison.   Christ, have mercy.

After the Christe, Bach sets the second Kyrie in antique style—as an intense Renaissance-style movement for voices and continuo bass. Except for the bass, the instruments have no independent role—they simply double the vocal parts. The conscious adoption of an archaic style for

Kryie II was common among Dresden composers; Bach, however, adds elements of emotional tension by employing fugue form (in which a primary theme is treated imitatively throughout the texture), choosing a tonality (F♯ minor) considered highly expressive by Baroque composers,[19] and creating a primary theme (the fugue subject) that moves sinuously by half steps. For added tension both subject and countersubject are treated in stretto—that is, the voices "butt in," creating overlapping statements of the theme. It is noteworthy that the fugue theme appears thirteen times—a phenomenon that may have symbolic intention in a movement constituting a desperate cry for mercy.

3. Chorus

Kyrie eleison.   Lord, have mercy.

Gloria

In the Gloria Bach abandons the reserve of the preceding Kyrie, expanding the vocal and instrumental sonority to the utmost. Trumpets and timpani play for the first time, and regular oboes replace the less powerful oboes d'amore, doubling the flute parts. The style is that of the concerto: a highly virtuosic interplay of voices and instruments, which places great technical demands on all performers, suggests a scene of majestic splendor.

George Stauffer observes:

> With the Gloria, we encounter an abrupt and shocking change of mood. Bright D major, the Baroque key of trumpets and drums, sweeps away the brooding B minor and F♯ minor of the Kyrie, extroverted concerto writing replaces introverted fugal development; and springy, dance-like rhythms, notated in the chamber meter of 3/8, supplant the *alla breve* gravity of Renaissance vocal style.[20]

With its origin in the angelic hymn occurring at Jesus' birth as recorded in the Gospel of Luke, the opening text has Christmas associations that are mirrored in Bach's treatment: the abrupt change of mood suggests the sudden appearance of the angels; the overt exuberance and dance-like triple meter suggest the nature of their news; the prominence of the trumpets, their heraldic function; and the rich texture (a total of sixteen independent vocal and instrumental parts), perhaps the numerical strength of the angel host. That Bach later reused this music in a cantata for Christmas Day (BWV 191) "leaves no doubt that he associated the score with the Nativity." The style of the movement is clearly instrumental; perhaps Bach adapted the music from a concerto movement that is no longer extant.

4. Chorus
Gloria in excelsis Deo.   Glory to God in the highest.

The shift to a contemplation of peace on earth occurs without a break. At the end of "Gloria in excelsis" the soprano voices were taken to their extreme upper register. Now most of the voices drop, the lines become more linear, the meter changes from sprightly triple groupings to a more sedate arrangement of four pulses per measure, and the trumpets and drums are hushed briefly. Lilting two-note groupings, sweet harmonies of parallel thirds and sixths, and sustained bass notes work together to create a pastoral atmosphere. After twenty measures the main theme becomes the subject of a fugue; a lively countersubject accompanies the primary melody, providing momentum. From the "lyricism of the Christmas Eve reminiscence" at the beginning of the movement, the music gradually intensifies until the "prophetic vision appears to be triumphantly fulfilled."[21]

5. (4.) Chorus
Et in terra pax hominibus bonae volun-   And on earth, peace to men of good will.
tatis.

For the centerpiece of the triptych with which the Gloria begins, Bach writes an aria in the florid operatic style, which may have been intended for the Dresden operatic mezzo-soprano Faustina Bordoni. Bach was evidently acquainted with Faustina (along with her husband, the composer Hasse). Her vocal technique was legendary, as the following description by the eighteenth-century writer Charles Burney attests.

> She in a manner invented a new kind of singing, by running divisions with a neatness and velocity which astonished all who heard her. . . . Her beats and trills were strong and rapid; her intonation perfect.[22]

Similarly, the Baroque theorist and flautist Johann Joachim Quantz (1697–1773) observed:

> Her execution was articulate and brilliant. She had a fluent tongue for pronouncing words rapidly and distinctly, and a flexible throat for

divisions, with so beautiful and quick a shake that she could put it in motion upon short notice, just when she would. The passages might be smooth, or by leaps, or consisting of iterations of the same tone, their execution was equally easy to her as to any instrument whatever.[23]

The solo violin part is likewise demanding. As for the other strings, they do not merely accompany but participate in the thematic unfolding of the movement.

6. (5.) Alto Aria

Laudamus te, benedicimus te, adoramus te, glorificamus te.	We praise you, we bless you, we worship you, we glorify you.

For the "Gratias" text, Bach chose to reuse a chorus from an earlier work—Cantata 29—where the words "Wir danken dir, Gott, und verkündigen deine Wunder" express the same prayerful homage as the Latin text of the mass. As in Kyrie II, Renaissance-style polyphony (now within the formal design of a double fugue) is used to set the text. The rising lines of the first theme appear in immediately overlapping fashion; the resulting dense web of sounds suggests the thickly intertwining trails of ascending incense. Then a second, more rhythmic subject is introduced on the words "propter magnam gloriam"; a subsequent combination of the two themes produces further intensification. Finally, "in a brilliant extension of the *stile antico* practice"[24] Bach adds additional instrumental lines to the four-voice vocal setting: first the second trumpet, then the first trumpet, and lastly the third trumpet with timpani, so that the movement climaxes in a blaze of glory.

7. (6.) Chorus

Gratias agimus tibi propter magnam gloriam tuam.	We give thanks to you for your great glory.

In the following love duet between God the Father and God the Son, Bach returns to the intimate, galant style of the "Christe" and "Laudamus te." Scored for obbligato flute, muted upper strings, and plucked cellos and basses, the duet features melodic lines that cascade downward, as if from heaven. The slurred note pairs of the instruments are often performed in reverse-dotted rhythm (the so-called Lombard rhythm), as was common in Dresden.

Bach's treatment of the text is noteworthy: two phrases (describing Father and Son, respectively) are presented more or less simultaneously—not, apparently, to shorten the movement but to emphasize the interaction between the two persons. Bach is not literal about the representation: the roles of Father and Son switch back and forth between soprano and tenor soloists. However, as Stauffer points out, "the first voice always carries the 'Domine Deus' line and the second the 'Domine Fili,' thus preserving the theological image of the Father preceding the Son."[25] Bach also adds a word ("altissime"—not normally part of the mass text) to the second text phrase, perhaps to allow better matching of the two text phrases by increasing the number of syllables in the latter.

8. (7.) Soprano and Tenor Duet

Domine Deus, Rex coelestis,	Lord God, King of Heaven,
Deus Pater omnipotens,	God the Father almighty.
Domine Fili unigenite,	Lord, the only begotten Son,
Jesu Christe altissime,	Jesus Christ, most high.
Domine Deus, Agnus Dei,	O Lord God, Lamb of God,
Filius Patris.	Son of the Father.

For the "Qui tollis" Bach adapted music from a work he had composed some twenty-five years earlier—the opening chorus of Cantata 46, *Schauet doch und sehet*. The appropriateness of Bach's choice is apparent from the similarity of affect between the original text and the new one. In Cantata 46 a verse from the book of Jeremiah's Lamentations ("Behold and see if there is any sorrow like my sorrow . . .") is applied Christologically to the Gospel lesson for the tenth Sunday after Trinity, which depicts Jesus weeping over Jerusalem's impending destruction. Bach's music, with its sighing and circling figures, monotonously plodding bass (whose throbbing cello rhythm is new to the mass setting), and harmonic dissonance effectively portrays a mood of resigned lament. It is therefore a good general match for the new text ("You who take away the sins of the world . . ."). Several of Bach's changes are illuminating. The new key is lower (B minor in place of the original D minor), serving to intensify the dark mood. The vigorous fugue with which the original setting concluded (on a suitably agitated text) now has no place, and is omitted. Finally, since the original chorus specifies only four voices, the vocal texture in the mass is reduced to that number. Bach does it, however, not by combining the two soprano parts but rather by omitting the higher of the two, an effect called for in only one other movement of mass—the "Crucifixus."

9. (8.) Chorus

Qui tollis peccata mundi, miserere nobis.	You who take away the sins of the world,
Qui tollis peccata mundi, suscipe depre-	have mercy upon us. You who take away
cationem nostram.	the sins of the world, receive our prayer.

Unlike Bach's other, shorter masses or masses by Dresden composers, the "Qui sedes" in the *Mass in B Minor* is set as an independent movement.

The scriptural context for the text has both Old Testament and New Testament roots: the words of the psalmist ("The Lord said unto my Lord, 'Sit thou at my right hand, until I make thine enemies thy footstool'"—Ps. 110:1) are reinterpreted according to the New Testament teaching of Christ's ascension ("So then after the Lord had spoken unto them, he was received up into heaven, and sat on the right hand of God."—Mark 16:19) and the doctrine of Christ as advocate at the right hand of God (Hebrews 8). After the lament of the "Qui tollis" (corresponding to Christ's Passion) this restrained and courtly dance movement (a gigue)—in which an oboe d'amore echoes the voice (effectively appearing "to the right of it") before joining with it in unison (i.e., the two are "of the same substance")—is evidently intended to suggest Christ's divine nature and his exalted position and role as mediator at the royal right hand of God.

10. (9.) Alto Aria

Qui sedes ad dextram Patris, miserere nobis.

You who sit at the right hand of God the Father, have mercy upon us.

The scoring of the "Quoniam" is extraordinary and unique. The movement calls for bass voice, natural horn (playing in a relatively high range), two bassoons (playing in thirds), and continuo bass. The contrast between the higher horn (which, along with the key of D major, had royal associations) and the other voices, all of them low, must surely have been inspired by the words, "tu solus altissimus Jesu Christe." With its determined ascending octave leap, the horn contributes an intense, magisterial presence, undoubtedly intended to symbolize Christ. Bach rarely wrote for obbligato bassoon; that he calls for *two* in this movement was probably because several virtuoso players were available in Dresden. The use of a hunting horn also points to Dresden, where it was a specialty.[26] Bach's unusual orchestration is further emphasized by the fact that two of the three obbligato instruments are unique to this movement: the corno da caccia and the second bassoon appear nowhere else in the entire mass.

The movement is cast in modified ternary form; Bach's attention to detail is evident in the fact that, when the opening material returns, Bach does not leave the expected ornamentation to the whims of the singer but writes out the embellishment.

11. (10.) Aria (Baritone)

Quoniam tu solus sanctus, tu solus Dominus, tu solus altissimus, Jesu Christe.

For you alone are holy; you alone are Lord; you alone, Jesus Christ, are most high.

The final movement of the Gloria, and one of exceptional virtuosity, follows without pause. While it had long been commonplace to clothe texts dealing with the Spirit "dynamically," Bach's setting of "cum sancto Spiritu" is particularly energetic. The overall design reveals five sections, which alternate between concertato style (instrumental and vocal bodies of sound placed in opposition to each other) and dense fugal writing, in which a leaping subject (derived from the material of the opening) is accompanied by an animated but more linear countersubject. To create a sense of forward motion Bach writes the first fugal exposition for voices alone (not counting the omnipresent continuo), then reinforces the vocal parts with instrumental doublings in the second one. To further energize the second exposition Bach creates "false" entries in stretto (the entries overlapping one another), leaving the listener guessing which of the statements will be completed. The overall effect is one of "feverish contrapuntal activity,"[27] which climaxes in the final seven measures when the sixteenth-note motion of first sopranos (doubled by the first violins, first oboe, and both flutes) passes to the first trumpet, whose sound radiates above the entire texture. Bach's own words, inscribed under the last measure of his manuscript, seem entirely fitting: "Fine—Soli Deo gloria" ("The End. To God alone be the glory.").[28]

12. (11.) Chorus

Cum Sancto Spiritu in gloria Dei Patris, amen.

With the Holy Ghost, in the glory of God the Father. Amen.

Symbolum Nicenum

For the Credo, Bach could not very well turn to Dresden models, for what few Credo settings existed were too short for his purpose. Written some fifteen years after the music of the Kyrie and Gloria, Bach's Credo (especially the opening movement) reflects his preoccupation with Renaissance-style polyphony in the intervening years. The overall structure is clearly symmetrical, with the centerpiece being the "Crucifixus." Bach's division of the text into individual movements is *not* commensurate with the text length but, apparently, with the relative significance of the text segments in Bach's estimation.

> It is clear that Bach intended from the outset to assign entire movements to the individual statements in the text that he believed the most significant, even if these often consisted of only a few words.[29]

A number of structural details suggest that Bach aimed to produce a highly integrated work, with "compelling transitions and cyclical allusions."[30] While perfectly chiastic, it is also developmental, following the three articles of Luther's Trinitarian division of the Creed. "That Bach was thinking along Lutheran lines . . . is verified by his label for the 'Et in unum Dominum' insert: 'Duo Voces Articuli 2': "The two vocal parts of Article 2.'"[31]

In the first movement Bach turned again to the antique church style, in which a theme is treated imitatively in all voices. It may well be that Bach's choice of style was motivated in part by a desire to portray the traditional text in an objective manner. The movement's musical theme is the chant intonation to the Credo used in Leipzig, and some part of it appears in every measure except the closing few. "In turning to a chant-derived theme and the sixteenth-century idiom of Palestrina, Bach acknowledged the roots of the Nicene Creed in the ancient church."[32] In all there are seven interwoven strands of melody in the counterpoint: five vocal parts and two violin lines. The resulting dense musical web is supported by a Baroque walking instrumental bass line, which adds an eighteenth-century instrumental touch to what is essentially a sixteenth-century style.[33]

1. (12.) Chorus
Credo in unum Deum.   I believe in one God.

In the "Patrem" Bach turned back to previously composed music: the opening chorus (a fugue) of Cantata 171, *Gott, wie dein Name, so ist auch dein Ruhm* ("According to thy name, O God, so is thy glory"). However, he made numerous clever adaptations: for example, to avoid emphasizing the division between the "Patrem" and the previous movement, he added material to the opening so that it begins in A major—even though the rest is in D. Bach also added declamatory "Credo" statements in the voices not preoccupied with the fugue theme. These, too, serve to unite the "Patrem" movement with the foregoing "Credo"; in addition, they perhaps pay homage to the so-called Credo Masses that were common in Dresden during Bach's time.[34]

The original cantata material is in four parts. Since Bach was apparently concerned about maintaining five-part vocal scoring throughout most of the mass (even reworking a four-voice cantata movement into five voices in the case of the "Et expecto"), it is initially surprising that he maintained the four-part vocal texture here. Upon closer examination, however, we see that, in both cantata and mass versions, an obbligato first trumpet line expands the fugal texture to five parts—perhaps Bach left it unaltered for this reason.

In Bach's symmetrical design, the first two movements of the Credo—the "Credo in unum Deum" and the "Patrem omnipotentem"—form an antique/modern style pair that is counterbalanced by another pair of movements at the end—the "Confiteor" and the "Et expecto." While the two movements are dissimilar in form and style it is clear that Bach wanted the components of the opening Credo sentence to be understood as inseparable. By using the venerated church style for the opening phrase ("Credo in unum Deum") he freed it from subjective associations. Accepted as dogma, it then becomes the basis for the second movement, which portrays the glorification of God as extending "to the ends of the earth" (as the original cantata model states it).[35]

2. (13.) Chorus
Patrem omnipotentem, factorem coeli et terrae, visibilium omnium et invisibilium.

The Father Almighty, maker of heaven and earth, and of all things visible and invisible.

The following love duet originally ended with the words "Et incarnatus est . . . et homo factus est." At some point, however, Bach decided to compose a new, self-contained movement for those words, apparently for the purpose of making the "Crucifixus" the centerpiece of a symmetrical arch. The decision entailed removing the "Et incarnatus" text from the duet without, however, shortening the music. Instead Bach kept the instrumental parts intact and reworked the vocal lines, redistributing the words over the entire musical span. Even with adjustments made to the vocal parts to accommodate the new text distribution, the process undermined the close relationship between text and music that had characterized the original version.[36] On the other hand, it highlighted the "Et incarnatus" text, which was now set as a self-contained movement.

The duet exhibits numerous symbolic features. Many writers have suggested that the two voices symbolize the second person of the Trinity (as they perhaps also do in the "Christe eleison"). In Helmuth Rilling's view,

> Bach expresses [the] simultaneous unity and difference between the Father and the Son in a single motive, which appears canonically in m. 1 in the highest orchestral parts and continues to pervade the entire movement. The notes of the motive are identical in both parts, a representation of the common substance of the Father and the Son. But the articulation is different, the last two eighths in the first part being marked staccato, while the same notes in the second part are slurred. The first motive, the stronger of the two, represents the all-powerful

Father; the second motive, a gentler musical gesture, represents the Son, who proceeds from the Father. This perfect musical synonym for the meaning of the text permeates the entire movement.[37]

3. (14.) Soprano and Alto Duet

Et in unum Dominum Jesum Christum, Filium Dei unigenitum et ex Patre natum ante omnia secula. Deum de Deo, lumen de lumine, Deum verum de Deo vero, genitum, non factum consubstantialem Patri, per quem omnia facta sunt. Qui propter nos homines, et propter nostram salutem descendit de coelis.

And in one Lord Jesus Christ, the only begotten Son of God, begotten of the Father before all ages, God of God, Light of Light, very God of very God, begotten, not made, of one substance with the Father, by whom all things were made. Who, for us men and for our salvation came down from heaven.

What follows is—despite its brevity—one of the most expressive pieces of the entire mass. Clearly symbolic are the imitative vocal lines (which descend as if coming down a staircase) and the sighing figures of the unison violin part (in whose jagged outline some writers perceive symbolic cross figures). Probably also symbolic are the many sharp signs, since the German word for sharp (*Kreuz*) simultaneously signifies "cross." A pulsating instrumental bass adds a hint of resignation and—because it sometimes repeats a single bass note many times before eventually finding resolution—expectation. In fact, all of the above musical elements combine to "create an atmosphere of anticipation—anticipation of the crucifixion that was made possible through Christ's incarnation."[38] The crucifixion, as portrayed in the following movement, is also foreshadowed in the alto line near the end of the "Et incarnatus," where we hear, in inverted form, the chromatic "lament" motive of the "Crucifixus." Immediately following this statement in the alto, the descending sighing/cross motive is presented in stretto (i.e., in overlapping fashion) in the two violin parts and the instrumental bass.

4. (15.) Chorus

Et incarnatus est de Spiritu sancto ex Maria virgine, et homo factus est.

And was incarnate by the Holy Spirit of the Virgin Mary, and was made man.

For the centerpiece of the Credo Bach adapted the opening chorus of his 1714 Weimar cantata "Weinen, Klagen, Sorgen, Zagen," BWV 12. The distinguishing musical feature of this movement is the "lamento bass," a bass line that descends by semitones from the tonic to the dominant. In the Baroque the figure was understood as a stereotypical gesture of lament, and was often used as a ground bass: a bass line that is continually repeated in a composition and thereby becomes the unifying element in the work. Bach presents the theme in throbbing quarter notes, thus heightening the sense of pathos and making this movement analogous to the "Qui tollis." A number of indicators suggest that this movement was very important in Bach's conception: its central position in a symmetrical structure, the use of ground bass (traditionally used for key texts), and the repetition of the entire text for emphasis. The ending—a musical extension that repeats the words "et sepultus est"—is particularly evocative with its chromatic harmonic language, low range and descending melodic movement, and subdued dynamic. Structurally, it accomplishes a modulation to G major, which allows the following movement ("Et resurrexit") to explode upon the listener's ear without pause.

5. (16.) Chorus

Crucifixus etiam pro nobis sub Pontio Pilato, passus et sepultus est.	Crucified also for us under Pontius Pilate, he suffered and was buried.

After the sepulchral ending of the "Crucifixus," the full orchestra (including trumpets and drums) erupts jubilantly in D major. The ascending figures are the antitheses of those in the preceding movement (especially noteworthy is the occasional ascending chromatic bass line, which approximates an inversion of the lamenting bass theme of the "Crucifixus"), and the overall effect suggests absolute confidence in the belief of the resurrection as described by Paul the apostle: "We shall all be changed, in a moment, in the twinkling of an eye, at the last trumpet. For the trumpet will sound, and the dead will be raised imperishable and we shall be changed."[39] Bach's writing is instrumental, and of a sufficiently virtuosic nature to suggest that he may have reused music from a now-lost concerto movement. "The switch from the primarily vocal idiom of the 'Et incarnatus' and the 'Crucifixus' to the unabashed instrumental style in the 'Et resurrexit' helps to produce the miraculous effect of euphoric awakening."[40] After a striking passage in which the vocal bass alone renders the text "And he shall come again, with glory, to judge both the quick and the dead," Bach repeats the opening music for the final phrase, "Whose kingdom shall have no end." This time, however, the trumpets dominate, and the "breathlessly ebullient" movement ends with a final triumphant flourish.

6. (17.) Chorus

Et resurrexit tertia die secundum scripturas; et ascendit in coelum, sedet ad dexteram Dei Patris, et iterum venturus est cum gloria judicare vivos et mortuos, cujus regni non erit finis.	And the third day he rose again according to the Scriptures; and ascended into heaven, and sits at the right hand of the Father. And he shall come again with glory to judge both the living and the dead, and his kingdom shall have no end.

In the following bass aria, Bach sets one of the longest text units in the Credo. The music reverts to the intimate style of such movements as the "Qui sedes." While the absence of close text-music relationships have led writers to conclude that this movement must be a parody of an earlier work, a connection between the general pastoral mood (created by the lilting dance meter, symmetrical phrases, sweet-sounding oboes d'amore, and consonant harmonies) and the textual image of the Holy Spirit is discernible.

7. (18.) Bass Aria

Et in Spiritum sanctum Dominum et vivificantem, qui ex Patre Filioque procedit; qui cum Patre et Filio simul adoratur et conglorificatur; qui locutus est per Prophetas. Et unam sanctam catholicam et apostolicam ecclesiam.	And I believe in the Holy Spirit, the Lord and giver of life, who proceeds from the Father and the Son; who together with the Father and the Son is adored and glorified; who spoke by the prophets. And I believe in one, holy, catholic, and apostolic Church.

The Credo concludes as it began, with a pair of choruses in contrasting (old versus modern) styles. The first of the two choral pillars, like its counterpart at the beginning of the Credo, is written in archaic motet style and, in the second half, cites a chant tune. Two distinct themes, one motto-like, the other motoric, are first developed independently, then combined. Again the chromatically rising bass theme (itself an inversion of the "lamento bass" heard in the "Crucifixus") appears. When Bach introduces the liturgical chant in measure 73, he does so in a structurally rigid manner, as if adding a further objective component. First the ancient tune appears in canon at the fifth between bass and alto, written in half notes with entrances one measure apart. In measure 92 the tenors sing it, now in longer (whole note) values. It is as if "Bach and his personal interpretation relinquish the place of importance to the objective affirmation of the Gregorian quotation."[41]

The movement ends with an eery rendition of the words "And I look for the resurrection of the dead," which will be repeated in the following movement. The fact that Bach chose to include the words here and repeat them at the beginning of the next movement is surely significant, especially in view of the fact that he apparently rejected a similar approach earlier when he decided to revise "Et unum Dominum" and make "Et incarnatus" an independent movement. (In that instance, he excised the "Et incarnatus" text from the end of "Et unum Dominum" and reworked the choral parts of the duet. It would have been much simpler to leave "Et in unum Dominum" as it was, then repeat the "Et incarnatus" text in the new movement.) Why did Bach follow a different course here? Perhaps he intended to make clear the connection between resurrection and baptism by having the words "Et expecto resurrectionem" follow on the heels of "unum baptisma in remissionem peccatorum." Perhaps he wanted to portray the tension inherent in Christian hope—a state conceptualized and expressed by theologians as "already . . . but not yet." Undoubtedly, by creating a bridge passage with a soft dynamic, slow tempo, and unstable harmonies (complete with reappearance of chromatically descending "Crucifixus" bass motive) he makes the jubilation of the following movement all the more abrupt, underscoring the suddenness of the event.

8. (19.) Chorus

Confiteor unum baptisma in remissionem peccatorum. Et expecto resurrectionem mortuorum.	I confess one baptism for the remission of sins. And I await the resurrection of the dead.

For the final movement of the Credo, Bach reworked a choral movement from his 1728 cantata "Gott, man lobet dich in der Stille," BWV 120, written for the inauguration of the Leipzig town council. His extensive revisions so completely altered the music that commentators did not recognize the connection until the twentieth century. One significant change is the vocal scoring: Bach expanded the four-voice original to five voices, so that it matches the scoring of the foregoing choral movements. Fanfare motives for the trumpets, soloistic timpani writing, ascending figures for "resurrectionem," and a developmental design serve to render the meaning of the words and to propel the music toward the substantial and ecstatic "Amen," which concludes not only the "Et expecto" but, "bound as it is to the prospect of eternal life, [also] the entire affirmation of the Credo."[42]

9. (20.) Chorus

Et expecto resurrectionem mortuorum et vitam venturi seculi, amen.	And I await the resurrection of the dead, and the life of the world to come. Amen.

Sanctus

Originating some twenty years earlier, the Sanctus is the oldest music in the *Mass in B Minor*. This fact helps account for its uniqueness: the orchestration requires no flutes but does call for a third oboe; the six-part vocal scoring is virtually unparalleled in Bach's output; within the mass itself no other movement uses polychoral texture (in which groups of voices and/or instruments respond to one another in an antiphonal manner) as a dominant structural principle.

The movement opens with a grand portrayal of the Isaiah text. The numbers 6 and 3 appear prominently—perhaps they are intended to function symbolically as Trinitarian references. At "Pleni sunt coeli" the texture abruptly changes, the accumulated inner tension of the amassed sound released in a fugue in 3/8 meter. Of this dramatic change Helmuth Rilling writes:

> Bach desired a contrast here: instead of the seventeen-part texture used up to now, one voice begins alone; instead of the carefully balanced and symbol-laden rhythms of the first section, the rhythmic character of the motivic material is light and lively. . . . The . . . countersubject . . . with its uninterrupted sixteenth-note coloratura, demonstrates even more clearly than the subject itself Bach's desire to write a virtuosic, "play-fugue."[43]

At the end Bach writes "a textbook-perfect example of a composed crescendo. All of the parts here begin in a relatively low range and move constantly upward for five measures. . . . The development of this crescendo culminates with the reentry of the trumpet-and-timpani-supported motive in the bass."[44]

1. (21.) Chorus

Sanctus, sanctus, sanctus Dominus Deus Sabaoth. Pleni sunt coeli et terra gloria ejus.	Holy, holy, holy Lord God of hosts. Heaven and earth are full of his glory.

Osanna, Benedictus, Agnus Dei, Dona nobis pacem

For the Osanna Bach expands the scoring to the limit. With eight-part choral writing (in double choir format) and the reentry of the flutes the texture now comprises a total of twenty parts—the most expansive in the entire Mass. The Benedictus, on the other hand, goes to the opposite extreme: with just three parts it represents the thinnest texture of the entire work. The Osanna is clearly related to the opening chorus of Bach's secular cantata "Preise dein Glücke, gesegnetes Sachesen," BWV 215; therefore either the Osanna is a reworking of BWV 215 or both were derived from a third now-lost work.

The Osanna's fast triple meter with upbeat suggests the passepied, a spirited court dance of French origin. Fortuitously, the borrowed material has a primary motive similar to the second subject of the "Pleni sunt coeli." This relationship helps connect the Osanna with the preceding Sanctus.

The Osanna is exuberant yet carefully structured. After an initial concerto-style opening the forces are reduced to chamber dimensions. Then begins a fugue-like development in which the motive works its way systematically (at two-measure intervals) through Choir I, Choir II (ascending from bass through soprano in Choir I; descending from soprano to bass in Choir II), and finally the orchestra (first the strings and woodwinds, then the trumpets). After a further section in which instrumental and vocal groups play off each other, the movement ends with instruments alone. "It is logical that the movement should end as it does with a purely instrumental section, given the previously observed transition from vocal to instrumental dominance within the movement."[45]

1. (22.) Chorus
Osanna in excelsis.   Hosanna in the highest.

In the Benedictus, we encounter the most intimate scoring of the entire mass: a solo tenor is accompanied by a treble instrument (unspecified in Bach's original but the part is perhaps most suitable for flute due to its range and tone color) and continuo. The variety of rhythms in the obbligato treble line imparts an improvisational character, typical of the "more pliant, flexible idiom" of the emerging *empfindsamer Stil* (the pre-Classical "sensitive style"), while the somewhat halting phrase structure of the tenor line suggests meditative restraint. Framed as it is by the two overtly exuberant Osanna statements, this movement "creates a very different world, one of solitary, almost mystical reflection."[46]

2. (23.)Tenor Aria   Blessed is He who comes in the name of
Benedictus qui venit in nomine Domini.   the Lord.

3. (-) Chorus (Repetition)
Osanna in excelsis.   Hosanna in the highest.

In the liturgy, the Agnus Dei is a threefold prayer just before the distribution of the bread and the wine of the Eucharist. In the *Mass in B Minor* Bach follows the Dresden custom of dividing the text into two separate movements. The threefold prayer is reduced to two and one-half statements—the concluding words, "Dona nobis pacem," lacking the introductory phrase "Agnus Dei, qui tollis peccata mundi." The most immediate reason for this structure is Bach's decision to create cyclical unity in the mass by bringing back the music of the "Gratias" for the "Dona nobis."

One could also argue, as Helmuth Rilling has done, that the closing ritornello (i.e., instrumental passage) of the Agnus Dei functions as a third
(non-verbal) statement of "Agnus Dei, qui tollis."

Bach's genius is once again evident in the music of this movement,
which, while taken from an earlier aria (reused by Bach also for an aria in
the *Ascension Oratorio*, BWV 11), displays much invention in its adaptation. A number of plaintive rhetorical figures help establish a mood of
intense supplication: dissonant, wrenching leaps (especially in the violins),
two-note slurred sighs (heard already in previous movements), and a
hypnotic walking bass of eighth notes separated by rests. The vocal theme
is echoed at the fifth by the violins playing in unison—as if they are
repeating the text rhetorically. The strict counterpoint, accompanied as it
is by the inflexible bass, produces an effect of still meditation (perhaps
even benumbed sadness), which finds some release at an interior pause—
the only instance within the entire work where a fermata appears within
a movement rather than on a final chord.

The five instrumental measures with which the Agnus Dei ends are
of utmost expressiveness, with unusual chromatic leaps that disorient the
listener with regard to the tonal center. Perhaps Bach wished to obscure
the ending of the Agnus Dei so that the "Dona nobis pacem," with its D-
major tonality and conjunct ascending lines, would stand out as much as
possible.[47]

4. (24.) Alto Aria
Agnus Dei qui tollis peccata mundi,   Lamb of God, who takes away the sins
miserere nobis.   of the world, have mercy upon us.

For the "Dona nobis" the music of the "Gratias" returns. That Bach chose
not to compose new music for the end of his work is surely significant.
Not only does the return of earlier material produce a sense of cyclical
unity, it also serves as a hermeneutical device, illuminating the new text.
While the words "Dona nobis pacem" are ordinarily heard as supplication,
they become here an assurance of prayer answered—a benediction. The
suppliants' anguished "miserere nobis" has been heard and peace is
assured. It is as if the great heavenly gates are opening slowly to receive
not just the prayer of the petitioners but the very suppliants themselves.

As before, Bach's expansion of the four-part contrapuntal texture with
three trumpet lines (after their initial role of simply doubling the voices)
produces an unexpected dynamic intensification: first the trumpets enter,
soaring high above the previous lines, and then, with a dramatic note of
finality, the timpani enters.

5. (25.) Chorus
Dona nobis pacem.   Grant us peace.

Notes

1. Translated Christoph Wolff, *New Bach Reader*, no. 162 (p. 158).
2. George B. Stauffer, *The Mass in B Minor* (New York: Schirmer Books, 1997; reprinted Yale University Press, 2003), 51.
3. John Butt, *Bach: Mass in B Minor* (Cambridge: Cambridge University Press, 1991), 14.
4. Anreas Bomba, CD booklet, J. S. Bach, *Mass in B Minor*, Gächinger Kantorei, Bach-Collegium Stuttgart (Helmuth Rilling, conductor), Hänssler CD 92.070, p. 32.
5. Yoshitake Kobayashi, trans. Jeffrey Baxter, "Universality in Bach's B Minor Mass: A Portrait of Bach in his Final Years (In Memoriam Dietrich Kilian)," *BACH: The Journal of the Riemenschneider Bach Institute* 24 (Fall/Winter 1993): 3–25.
6. Georg von Dadelsen, "Bach's h-Moll Messe," *Über Bach und anderes. Aufsätze und Vorträge 1957–1982* (Laaber: Laaber, 1983): 139; trans. in Stauffer, *Mass in B Minor*, 256.
7. Christoph Wolff, "Bach the Cantor, the Capellmeister, and the Musical Scholar: Aspects of the B-Minor Mass," *The Universal Bach. Lectures Celebrating the Tercentenary of Bach's Birthday* (Philadelphia: American Philosophical Society, 1986), 45; cited in Stauffer, *Mass in B Minor*, 257.
8. Butt, *Bach: Mass in B Minor*, 102.
9. Stauffer, *Mass in B Minor*, 257–58.
10. Stauffer, *Mass in B Minor*, 19–23.
11. See Christoph Wolff, Origins of the Kyrie of the B Minor Mass, *Bach. Essays on His Life and Music* (Cambridge, Mass.: Harvard University Press, 1991), 141–51; Stauffer, *Mass in B Minor*, 54.
12. See Wolff, "Origins of the Kyrie," 147–48; Robin A. Leaver, "Bach and the German Agnus Dei" in *A Bach Tribute. Essays in Honor of William H. Scheide* (published simultaneously in the United States and Germany. Kassel: Bärenreiter; Chapel Hill: Hinshaw Music; 1993), 163. Luther based both his Kyrie and the so-called German Agnus Dei ("Christe du Lamm Gottes") on the traditional first psalm tone. See Wolff, "Origins of the Kyrie," 147; Robin A. Leaver, "Liturgical Chant Forms in Bach's Compositions for Lutheran Worship: A Preliminary Survey," *Die Quellen Johann Sebastian Bachs – Bachs Musik im Gottesdienst*. Proceedings of the Symposium of the Internationale Bachakademie Stuttgart, 1995 (Heidelberg: Manutius, 1998), 418, 425; Robin A. Leaver, "Luther and Bach, the 'Deutsche Messe' and the Music of Worship," *Lutheran Quarterly*, 15 (2001): 331.
13. Wolff, "Origins of the Kyrie," 147.

14. Leaver, "Bach and the German Agnus Dei," 163; Leaver, "Luther and Bach," 331; Robin A. Leaver, "The Mature Vocal Works and Their Theological and Liturgical Context," in *The Cambridge Companion to Bach*, ed. John Butt (Cambridge: Cambridge University Press, 1997), 112.

15. Stauffer, *Mass in B Minor*, 56.

16. Stauffer, *Mass in B Minor*, 53.

17. The first number follows the numbering system used in the new critical edition of Bach's works: *Johann Sebastian Bach: Neue Bach-Ausgabe sämtlicher Werke (NBA)*, ed. Johann-Sebastian-Bach-Institut Göttingen, and Bach-Archiv Leipzig (Leipzig and Kassel, 1954–). The second number (in parentheses) follows the system used in the *Bach-Werke-Verzeichnis* (BWV); see Wolfgang Schmieder, *Thematisches Verzeichnis der musikalischen Werke von Johann Sebastian Bach*, rev. and expanded ed. (Wiesbaden: Breitkopf and Härtel, 1990).

18. The unison violin line reinforces the sense of happy concord. Stauffer, *Mass in B Minor*, 57.

19. Stauffer, *Mass in B Minor,* 62.

20. Stauffer, *Mass in B Minor*, 64.

21. Rilling, *B-minor Mass*, 24.

22. Charles Burney, *A General History of Music from the Earliest Ages to the Present* (London, 1789), with critical and historical notes by Frank Mercer (New York: Dover, 1957), 2:738.

23. Johann Joachim Quantz cited by Charles Burney, *A General History of Music*, 2:745.

24. Rilling, *B-minor Mass*, 28.

25. Stauffer, *Mass in B Minor*, 79.

26. For example, high florid horn parts appear frequently in mass settings by Johann David Heinichen (1683–1729) and Jan Dismas Zelenka (1679–1745). See Stauffer, *Mass in B Minor*, 90–91. Stauffer also notes that in the Dresden performing parts of Bach's work the horn part "is written on a separate sheet of paper, which leads one to believe that Bach intended it for a specialist rather than an unoccupied trumpet player."

27. Stauffer, *Mass in B Minor*, 94.

28. Rilling, *B-minor Mass*, 43, 47, 48.

29. Rilling, *B-minor Mass*, 52.

30. Stauffer, *Mass in B Minor*, 141.

31. Stauffer, *Mass in B Minor*, 144; see also 99.

32. Stauffer, *Mass in B Minor*, 103.

33. Stauffer, *Mass in B Minor*, 100.

34. Stauffer, *Mass in B Minor*, 109.

35. See also Rilling, *B-minor Mass*, 63.

36. Rilling, *B-minor Mass*, 68.

37. Rilling, *B-minor Mass*, 64.

38. Stauffer, *Mass in B Minor*, 116.

39. 1 Corinthians 15:51–52, Revised Standard Version.

40. Stauffer, *Mass in B Minor*, 127.

41. Rilling, *B-minor Mass*, 99.
42. Rilling, *B-minor Mass*, 110.
43. Rilling, *B-minor Mass*, 124.
44. Rilling, *B-minor Mass*, 128.
45. Rilling, *B-minor Mass*, 139.
46. Stauffer, *Mass in B Minor*, 162.
47. Rilling, *B-minor Mass*, 148.

Bibliography

Bomba, Andreas. "Opus summum-opus ultimum, Bach's *Mass in B Minor*." CD booklet. J. S. Bach, *Mass in B Minor*. Gächinger Kantorei Stuttgart, Bach-Collegium Stuttgart (Helmuth Rilling, conductor). Hänssler 92.070.

Boyd, Malcolm, ed. *Oxford Composer Companions: J. S. Bach*. Oxford: Oxford University Press, 1999.

Braun, Werner. "Passion. 6. Eighteenth Century." In *New Grove Dictionary of Music and Musicians*. 2d ed. Vol. 19. Ed. Stanley Sadie. London: Macmillan, 2001.

Burney, Charles. *A General History of Music from the Earliest Ages to the Present* (London, 1789) with critical and historical notes by Frank Mercer. New York: Dover, 1957.

Butt, John. *Bach: Mass in B Minor*. Cambridge: Cambridge University Press, 1991.

———. "St. John Passion." In *Oxford Composer Companions: J. S. Bach*, edited by Malcolm Boyd. Oxford: Oxford University Press, 1999.

David, Hans T., and Arthur Mendel, eds. *The New Bach Reader: A Life of Johann Sebastian Bach in Letters and Documents*. Revised and enlarged by Christoph Wolff. New York: W. W. Norton, 1998.

Dean, Winton. "Bordoni, Faustina." In *New Grove Dictionary of Music and Musicians*. 2d ed. Vol. 3. Ed. Stanley Sadie. London: Macmillan, 2001.

Dürr, Alfred. *Die Kantaten von Johann Sebastian Bach mit ihren Texten*. 2 vols. Kassel: Bärenreiter, 1985.

Geck, Martin. Trans. Stewart Spencer. CD booklet. J. S. Bach, *Johannes-Passion*. Concentus musicus Wien (Nikolaus Harnoncourt, conductor). Teldek 9031–74862–2.

Hochreither, Karl. Trans. Melvin P. Unger. *Performance Practice of the Instrumental-Vocal Works of Johann Sebastian Bach*. Lanham, Md.: Scarecrow Press, 2002.

Leaver, Robin A. "Bach and the German Agnus Dei." In *A Bach Tribute. Essays in Honor of William H. Scheide*. Published simultaneously in the United States and Germany. Kassel: Bärenreiter; Chapel Hill, N. C.: Hinshaw Music, 1993, 163–71.

———. "Liturgical Chant Forms in Bach's Compositions for Lutheran Worship: A Preliminary Survey." In *Die Quellen Johann Sebastian Bachs – Bachs Musik im Gottesdienst*. Proceedings of the Symposium of the Internationale Bachakademie Stuttgart, 1995. Heidelberg: Manutius, 1998, 417–28.

———. "Luther and Bach, the 'Deutsche Messe' and the Music of Worship." *Lutheran Quarterly* 16 (2001): 317–35.

———. "Mature Vocal Works and their theological and liturgical Context, The." In *The Cambridge Companion to Bach*, ed. John Butt. Cambridge: Cambridge University Press, 1997, 86–122.

———. "Passion." In *Oxford Composer Companions: J. S. Bach*, ed. Malcolm Boyd. Oxford: Oxford University Press, 1999.

Marissen, Michael. *Lutheranism, Anti-Judaism, and Bach's St. John Passion*. New York: Oxford University Press, 1998.

Metcalf, Marion Metcalf. "J. S. Bach: *Johannes Passion*." March 11, 2000. Notes for the Alexandria Choral Society's 1985 performance of the *St. John Passion*, reprinted in remembrance of Marion R. Metcalf, formerly a member of the society. http://www.alexchoral society.org/bachnotes.htm (accessed June 23, 2004).

Neumann, Werner, and Hans-Joachim Schulze, eds. *Bach-Dokumente*. 4 vols. Leipzig: Bach-Archiv, 1963, 1969, 1972, 1979.

Rilling, Helmuth. Trans. Gordon Paine. *Johann Sebastian's B-minor Mass*. Princeton, N. J.: Prestige Publications, 1984.

———. "Helmuth Rilling on *St. Matthew Passion*." CD booklet. J. S. Bach, *St. Matthew Passion*. Gächinger Kantorei Stuttgart, Bach-Collegium Stuttgart (Helmuth Rilling, conductor). CBS M3K 79403.

———. Trans. Kenneth Nafziger. *J. S. Bach St. Matthew Passion*. New York: C. F. Peters, 1975.

Schmieder, Wolfgang. *Thematisches Verzeichnis der musikalischen Werke von Johann Sebastian Bach*. Rev. & expanded ed. Wiesbaden: Breitkopf & Härtel, 1990.

Spencer, Stewart. CD booklet, libretto translation. J. S . Bach, *St. Matthew Passion*, Gabrieli Consort (Paul McCreesh, conductor). Archiv 474 200-2.

Stauffer, George B. *The Mass in B Minor*. New York: Schirmer Books, 1997.

Wolff, Christoph. *Bach. Essays on His Life and Music*. Cambridge, Mass.: Harvard University Press, 1991.

Wong, Audrey, and Norm Proctor. "St. John Passion." July 7, 2003. http://www.bcg.org/Program_Notes/StJohn_694.html (accessed June 24, 2004).

Glossary

adagio. In a slow tempo.

aria. A self-contained lyrical vocal solo with instrumental accompaniment in a work of operatic style.

arpeggio. A chord whose tones are played in succession rather than simultaneously.

canon. A composition or passage of music in which a melody is imitated by one or more voices in a highly structured way (i.e., at a fixed interval of pitch and time).

cantus firmus. An existing melody, which is incorporated structurally in a musical composition.

chorale. A German Protestant hymn.

chromatic. The opposite of diatonic. Related to the tones or harmonies not normally associated with a particular musical scale or key.

coloratura. Vocal music characterized by passages of florid ornamentation. A singer (especially a soprano) with the requisite range and agility to sing such passages.

concerto. An instrumental form in which an instrument or group of instruments is placed in musical opposition to a larger group of instruments.

continuo. Abbreviation of *basso continuo*. The foundational bass line of a baroque composition with its accompanying harmonies, which are realized usually on a keyboard instrument.

corno da caccia. Hunting horn.

da capo. From the beginning. Often used in relation to baroque arias consisting of two contrasting sections followed in performance by a repetition of the first section.

diatonic. The opposite of chromatic. Related to the tones and harmonies that employ only the degrees of the major and minor scales (i.e., without the intervening notes).

fermata. A pause. The prolongation of a tone, chord, or rest. A sign used to indicate such a prolongation.

fugue. An imitative musical passage or composition in which a distinctive theme is treated successively by participating voices according to prescribed procedures.

ground bass. A bass line that is continually repeated in a musical composition.

key. A system of notes whose relationships amongst each other identify one particular note as the primary one (the "home base"). The word "tonality" is also used in this way.

melisma. A musical passage in which several (or many) notes accompany individual text syllables. Adjective: melismatic.

modulation. A transition from one key (tonality) to another.

monophony. A style of musical composition consisting of a single melodic line.

obbligato. An independent, indispensable accompanying melodic line in a musical composition.

oboe da caccia. An alto oboe of the baroque, curved in shape, precursor of the English horn.

oboe d'amore. A baroque oboe pitched a minor third below the modern oboe.

oratorio. A narrative or dramatic composition of considerable length in operatic style, usually on a sacred theme, and not intended to be staged.

parody. A reworked version of an already established composition. The process of borrowing and reworking material in this way.

passacaglia. A musical form of the seventeenth and eighteenth centuries consisting of continuous variations over a repeated bass line.

piccardy third. The major third of a final chord in a passage that is written in a minor key.

pizzicato. For stringed instruments normally played with a bow, an indication that the strings are to be plucked with a finger.

polyphony. A composition or passage of music comprised of multiple simultaneous melodic parts. The word "counterpoint" is also used in this way.

recitative. A vocal passage in a work of operatic style in which the text is declaimed in a manner approximating the inflection and emphasis of natural speech.

ritornello. An instrumental interlude, often repeated. In a concerto, such
   a passage for full orchestra.
stretto. A fugal technique in which statements of the theme overlap to
   produce increasing tension.
syncopation. A shift of accent so that a note normally falling on an
   unaccented beat within its metrical scheme receives emphasis.
tonality. See key.
viola da gamba. A bass viol, held between the legs. Like other members
   of the viol family it has a fretted fingerboard and six strings.
viola d'amore. A treble viol with sympathetic strings, that is, strings that
   are not played but reinforce the sound of the played strings by
   vibrating along with them.

Index of Movements

Note: The first number follows the numbering system used in the new critical edition of Bach's works (*Neue Bach-Ausgabe*). The second number (in parentheses) follows the system used in the *Bach-Werke-Verzeichnis* (BWV).

About the Author

Melvin Unger is professor of music at Baldwin-Wallace College Conservatory of Music in Berea, Ohio, where he serves as director of the Riemenschneider Bach Institute and holds the Riemenschneider Chair in Music History and Literature. As director of the institute he acts as editor-in-chief of the journal *Bach*, and he serves as administrative head of the Riemenschneider Bach Library and the annual Baldwin-Wallace Bach Festival. The author of a number of scholarly articles and music editions, he has also published three previous books: *The German Choral Church Compositions of Johann David Heinichen (1683–1729)*, *Handbook to Bach's Sacred Cantata Texts: An Interlinear Translation with Reference Guide to Biblical Quotations and Allusions*, and *Performance Practice of the Instrumental-Vocal Works of Johann Sebastian Bach* (a revised translation of Karl Hochreither's *Zur Aufführungs-praxis der Vokal-Instrumentalwerke Johann Sebastian Bachs*).

Active as a choral conductor, Professor Unger directs the Baldwin-Wallace Singers and the Singers' Club of Cleveland, a male chorus founded in 1891. His choral groups have appeared at conventions and festivals in Canada, the United States, and Europe.

Date Due

DEC 0 9 2006			